# THE STING OF THE
# SERPENT'S BLADE

GENEVIEVE MCKAY

StonePony Studios

## Chapter 1

*Beep. Beep. Beep.* The alarm went off before the crack
of dawn; interrupting the first good dream I'd had
in months. There'd been no death, no ghosts and no rivers of
blood. Just Gil and I lying peacefully on a warm beach next to
a blue, tropical sea.

I swiped resentfully at the ancient alarm clock before
burrowing back under the covers, pulling them firmly over my
head to keep off the winter chill.

Greystone manor had been in my family for well over two
hundred years and had hardly been updated in all that time. It
was a beautiful house but it was also oversized, drafty and
damp. There was no central heating, which was quite the hard-
ship when you were in the middle of a cold, Canadian winter.
Even with the embers of last night's fire still burning low in the
fireplace, my room was freezing.

I was already missing my happy dream. There had been
sun, and palm trees and no one to bother us. Why on earth
had the alarm gone off so early?

From under the blankets, I heard a soft thumping noise in
the far corner of the room as if a large animal had brushed

clumsily up against my dresser. It was followed by the gentle *tok tok tok* that was the now-familiar sound of a horse walking stealthily across a hardwood floor.

"Bally, go away," I mumbled as the covers near my shoulder lifted a little and then dropped down again. "It's too early for our walk. Go back to bed."

There was silence and then a soft *whuffling* next to my ear, followed by a puff of warm breath that worked its way right through the blankets to my skin.

Muttering all sorts of dire threats, I squirmed away but it was no use. Whenever Bally was bored of life in the stables, he came to find me. And now that he was, well, *on the other side*, there were no walls, borders, or barriers that could keep him out. It was a good thing he was so darn cute.

"Fine." I sat up and threw the covers off all at once, like ripping off a Band-Aid.

Morris, the ex-barn cat, who had also been sleeping under the blankets, blinked in astonishment as the surge of cold air ruffled his orange fur. With a dark look in Bally's direction, he squashed himself under my pillows, clearly not ready to face the day yet.

I climbed from the oversized four-poster bed, walking on my heels and curling my toes to avoid the icy floorboards. Hobbling to my dresser, I threw on thick winter socks and then layered fleece-lined breeches, two thermal shirts, and a sweater over top.

The choice to wear riding clothes was a bit ironic since I still hadn't gotten on a horse since the night I'd been shot. The night Bally had been killed. That moment was seared into my mind permanently.

Technically, after five months of rest, my bullet-torn arm was pretty much healed. It was often sore, and it had scars, but it was functional, and I knew in my heart that the pain wasn't enough to stop a real athlete. Someone who wasn't a quitter.

I pulled my hair back into a ponytail and surveyed my reflection critically in the mirror, taking in my messy blonde hair and the winter-pale complexion that made my freckles stand out more than usual. I rubbed my right arm reflexively, feeling the small indents even through my sweater. The bullet holes were now just pale, pink depressions; one on the top side of my arm where the bullet had gone in and one on the bottom where it had exited again. I only wished that my mental scars had healed as nicely as my physical ones.

Bally looked at me expectantly, his silver coat translucent in the soft glow of the dying fire. When he'd been alive, I'd kept his mane neatly trimmed and his coat clipped short. But after he'd died, his mane had grown to halfway down his shoulder and he'd developed the soft, fluffy coat of a wild horse in winter. I wasn't sure if this was something he'd chosen to do or if it had just happened; I hadn't worked out all the details of this ghost thing yet.

Now he bobbed his pearly grey nose up and down, encouraging me like I was about to hand him a treat for hauling me out of bed.

"No snacks for you, ghost-horse," I said, stifling a yawn. "Why are you up so early anyway?"

Suddenly I remembered, *my interview*. That's why I'd set the alarm to go off before sunrise. I was on my way to landing my first real job.

Despite living in a fancy house and having a stable full of well-bred horses at my fingertips, I barely had any money of my own. It wasn't like my mother paid me a salary to ride her horses. And any meager show winnings I'd once earned had long ago dried up. I was running out of capital at an alarming rate.

In a fit of desperation, I'd carefully drafted and handed out résumés to half the businesses in our little town. Something I would have never dared to do six months ago.

I'd gotten exactly one response and that was from a popular local café called MapleBrew. I had zero experience in sales or, uh, serving, but I was hopeful that I could learn on the job if they would just give me a chance.

"Come on, Bally," I said. "We only have time for a quick walk today. I still have to get my chores done."

He snorted agreeably and headed down the wide hallway at a brisk trot, his plump hindquarters swaying from side to side, making me laugh. Having a horse in the house, even a ghost-horse, was a joy that never got old.

He made a great show of clattering down the huge wooden staircase that bisected our house in half, rocking right back on his hocks and doing a series of noisy courbettes, or tiny hops, down the steps like a Lipizzaner until he reached the ground floor. It was a good thing nobody but me could hear the racket he made.

Actually, since Mother and her entourage had abandoned ship, there weren't many people left to hear him anyway. Besides our cook Betty, it was just me, the ghosts and Morris rambling around in the massive old house. All the rest of the help disappeared to their own places around the property the second their workdays were done. It wasn't like anyone was dying to stick around and spend any more time with me than they had to.

"Show off," I told Bally, throwing on a thick coat, boots, woolly mittens, and a voluminous toque and scarf combo that covered my entire head until only my eyes were showing. As soon as I was fully suited up, we headed out the side kitchen door into the frosty pre-dawn morning.

It had snowed hard overnight and some of the new drifts were well over my knees. A fat glowing moon sat low on the horizon, bright enough to cast the world around me in a magical, silvery light.

I tromped along the driveway, already puffing hard with the effort just to lift my heavy boots through the snow. At the bottom of the lane, we turned right and headed up the hill toward the scenic lookout spot that Bally liked best. I wasn't sure if it was because it had been our favourite place to go together when he'd been alive or if there was something else that drew him in that direction. But, every morning like clockwork, he headed this way on our pre-breakfast walk.

The light from my headlamp lit up the areas the moon couldn't reach, bouncing off drifts and snow-laden trees and reflecting weird shadows on the snowy path ahead of us. While I trudged breathlessly through the snow, Bally cavorted alongside me effortlessly like a large, silver shadow, his eyes shining as he leapt and bucked excitedly through the icy landscape.

When we reached the top of the hill, he stopped and lifted his head, whickering softly as he turned to survey the landscape stretched out below.

I plunked myself down in a deep snowdrift beside him and stared up at the last few stars in the sky, contemplating the twists and turns my life had taken in the last few months. Despite all the reasons I'd had to want to leave this place, I still felt a fierce, overwhelming love for it that caught me off guard in moments like this. Greystone was a part of me somehow, right to the bone.

I didn't even feel like the same person as when I'd left Greystone back in September. So much had happened that I felt like it had been six years ago rather than six months.

Murder, kidnapping and exposing nasty family secrets had a way of aging a person.

The biggest change that had happened to me had been

recovering not only a bunch of my repressed childhood memories but also the gift I'd almost lost; my ability to see ghosts.

In all the drama that had unfolded at Dark Lady Farm, I'd discovered my mother had paid some creepy family doctor to suppress my gift to see spirits when I was a teenager. A procedure that also had the benefit of squashing my rebellious nature and making it easier for her to order me around. Very convenient for her.

Mother's excuse was that the procedure had been done for my own good. So, I could fit in better at school, and removing my ability to see spirits might make room for better gifts to manifest. Gifts like her own precognition that could benefit Greystone and make yet more money for our already wealthy family.

I wasn't buying it for a second though. My mother never made any decisions unless they benefitted herself. Unfortunately, for her, no other gifts had manifested in me. And I'd spent years living a half-life, locked away from the parts of myself that brought me joy.

Mother had completely washed her hands of me when Gil and I had come back from Dark Lady Farm; battered, broken and spitting mad at what she'd done to me, to *us*, all those years ago.

I'd been dealing with not only the abrupt return of my gift, and the murder of Bally, but also years' worth of suppressed emotions and memories. I wasn't the mild-mannered pushover she'd come to expect anymore. And a daughter who argued all the time, who refused to ride and who saw ghosts was no use to her at all.

And it wasn't like she was going to do anything crazy like apologize or admit that she'd been wrong.

It had been a relief when she'd hightailed it for her sister's estate in Patagonia for the winter season, dragging my poor father and nearly all the household staff with her.

"Since you're determined to blame me for everything that's gone wrong in your life, Jillian," my mother had said haughtily, "I will leave you to run Greystone by yourself so you can see all the sacrifices your father and I make daily on your behalf."

Only a few of the older staff members who were no longer fit to travel stayed behind. Mr. and Mrs. Hopps, the married chauffeur and head housekeeper who lived in the stone cottage at the far end of the property refused to go. And our old cook Betty had elected to stay behind as well. Mother had grumbled that they were abandoning her in her hour of need, but they'd all been with the family since before I was born so there wasn't much she could do to force them on a twenty-hour flight halfway around the world.

"I wasn't about to leave my home to travel to lord-knows-where at a moment's notice," Betty had grumbled to me privately. "And I wasn't about to leave you alone to fend for yourself either."

Also left behind, as assistants to the elderly Mrs. Hopps, were two Dutch, or Swiss, or maybe Icelandic girls who had identical blonde braids, freckles, and who didn't speak a word of English. They might have been sisters but I had no idea. Whenever anyone looked at them, they fell to giggling hysterically and had to leave the room. They drove Mother crazy anyway so she'd been happy to leave them at Greystone.


Far below, the lights in the training barn came on and I sat up, pulling myself out of my brooding thoughts and back to reality. Christoph or one of the grooms must have arrived to start the morning chores.

*I wish it was Gil down there*, I thought wistfully. My best friend, and on-again-off-again love interest, had been away for the last two months at a fancy dressage barn down south. He'd accepted a short internship with a famous trainer, a former Olympian, and we'd sent along our Oldenburg stallion, Coconut, for extra training too.

I missed Gil like crazy but it had been too good of an opportunity for him to pass up. And, no matter how much it killed me, it was better if we had some time apart to figure our complicated relationship out.

On the night Bally had been killed, in the middle of all that chaos, blood and trauma, I'd finally declared my undying love for Gil. Something that had been years overdue.

But we didn't get to play out a happy love story. Instead, Gil had confessed that my mother had bribed and threatened him to be my friend when I was a child, something that had carried on until we were adults. A confession that had broken my heart.

The revelation hadn't changed the way we felt about each other, not deep down, but trust had been broken and we needed to figure out how to find our way forward.

Bally nickered under his breath, probably thinking about all that delicious hay and grain being served up for the other, living, horses. I was still figuring out how the whole ghost thing worked, but I'd noticed that food still excited him and that he still went through the motions of eating. And it was funny, but I could have sworn that the hay and grain I faithfully put out for him every day looked to have been nibbled at when I came to clear it away.

The grooms, understandably, thought I was completely nuts for putting food and bedding in an empty stall for a dead horse.

From the outside, it must have seemed like I'd lost my ever-loving mind. But, no matter how crazy it looked, I just couldn't give it up. Bally stared at me so expectantly when the other horses were fed that there was no way I could disappoint him.

He'd died saving my life and I owed him everything; putting food out for him was the least I could do.

"We should get back, buddy," I said, chafing my hands together to warm them up. "You have horse things to do and I have a job interview to get ready for."

Walking downhill went much faster than our uphill trek had. Despite his excitement about breakfast, Bally stayed right beside me the whole way, occasionally reaching out a nose to steady me when I slid on the icy patches.

Unfortunately, even though I could see Bally as clear as day, I couldn't touch him. If I tried, my hand sank right through his body; something I avoided as much as possible since the cold, squelchy feeling creeped me out. But he could touch *me* if he felt like and sometimes he bumped into things or could move objects. The other day he'd been searching for a snack in the kitchen and had knocked a bowl of sugar right off the table in front of Betty. It had scared her nearly to death when the bowl had randomly shattered to the floor in front of her.

Nanny had told me that this ability was very unusual for a newly made ghost and that Bally was particularly strong for some reason. Older spirits could make things move occasionally, but it took a lot of effort and often left them weak afterward. Not Bally though; he was special.

## Chapter 2

The barn lights blazed in the early morning darkness, spilling out from the wide aisleway into the snowy courtyard. Despite the early hour and the biting cold, a shiver of pleasure went through me when I stepped inside.

The horses nearest the door looked up when Bally and I came in, calling out for their breakfast. Allison, the bossy bay mare who was one of my charges, pinned her ears at Bally and squealed under her breath, tossing her big head up and down in irritation. She was all show though because as soon as Bally went fearlessly up to sniff noses, her ears perked back up and she nickered lovingly at him. She ran a little hot and cold with her friendships.

I wasn't sure if all the horses could see Bally; some of them just ignored him completely and some, like Allison, seemed to consider him to be just another normal horse. A few would snort like they were afraid and made it clear that they didn't want him too close. But others, like my little colt Damascus, loved him. Before the weather had turned nasty, Bally and Damascus had spent hours together in the pasture, playing and grazing nose to nose like the best of friends.

"Ready for your breakfast, guys?" I asked to the sea of eager faces.

They bobbed their noses and nickered to me, hurrying me on my way.

"All right, sit tight everyone, your hay is coming."

Ahead of Alastair halting my riding career with his well-placed bullet, I'd been responsible for riding and showing five of the Greystone horses, including Bally. And I'd been expected to ride some of the up-and-coming youngsters for Christoph as well. It hadn't been unusual for me to ride seven or eight horses a day, six days a week. But I'd never been allowed to care for them before.

My mother had strict ideas about maintaining a firm distance between staff and family. Employees were supposed to know their place (at the bottom) and we were supposed to know ours (at the top). And those lines were not to be blurred.

As a child, I'd fought hard against these arbitrary rules. I'd loved horses and wanted to take care of them myself like the kids in the pony-books I read did. I didn't mind getting dirty or doing hard work.

She'd finally, reluctantly, given in on letting me groom my horses but I'd never been allowed to clean stalls, sweep or help at feeding time. Even when I'd tried to pitch in, the grooms had anxiously shooed me away. They risked getting fired if my mother had caught me with a broom in my hand.

But all that had changed this winter, pretty much the second my parent's plane took off. With Gil away and a dire shortage of stable help, everyone on the farm had to take on extra work if we wanted to stay afloat. Including me.

It was hard work but I loved every second of it. I shovelled my stalls and fed meals four times a day, cleaned tack, swept the aisles and chipped ice out of the water buckets. And of course, I kept my horses groomed and exercised and made sure they didn't fall too far behind in their training. Even though I wasn't riding, I could lunge them and do groundwork.

Every horse in the barn except Bally and Damascus was for sale. Even in the dead of winter, it was common to get a phone call from someone looking for dressage prospects, so it was important to keep all the horses ready for inspection. We might be in the middle of nowhere, but our breeding and training program was respected all across North America and even overseas.

Under my care, I had Lark, a flashy dark mare with a star on her forehead and white stockings that went up over her knees; she just needed a few more show miles this spring before she could command the big prices Mother was asking for her. Serena was a gentle grey mare who hadn't really lived up to her amazing bloodlines but would probably make a great junior or amateur horse. Lilo was a funny red gelding with a crooked blaze who loved to play tricks like tipping over the wheelbarrow when you were attempting to clean his stall. He also liked to grab the hose when you were filling his bucket and spray water everywhere. You couldn't take your eyes off him for a second without him attempting some sort of shenanigans.

And then there was Allison, a blood-bay mare who was becoming more of a handful every day that she sat idle. If I'd thought keeping them all fit had been a full-time job before, it was ten times the work now that I was the sole person responsible for their care.

The rear door to the barn rolled back with a rumble and the rest of the stable-hands began to arrive, shivering in the frigid February air despite being wrapped from head to toe in patch-work winter gear. None of our staff were locals and many of them came from much warmer climates, so adjusting to Canadian winters sometimes took them a while. Some of them never adjusted at all.

Besides Gil and Christoph, we had five grooms. Well, they

were called grooms but they didn't get to just brush and ride horses. They were expected to do all the heavy labour as well. Mother lured them to Greystone with the bright promise of working with our first-class horses. When they arrived, they found low pay, poor living conditions, and fourteen-hour gruelling workdays in all sorts of weather.

None of them lasted more than a season or two before they abandoned ship, and lately, I'd wondered if maybe that's why my mother treated them so badly. The shorter their stay, the less likelihood of anyone finding out her family secrets.

"Morning," they mumbled to me one by one in passing as they headed to throw their impatient charges hay and then fill up their coffee mugs in the tack room.

I didn't know any of this crew very well. They all worked hard, long hours in the freezing cold and didn't have much energy for anything else. They were housed together in the dilapidated staff accommodations behind the barn and had developed a tight comradery with one another that I never seemed to be a part of, though Gil and Christoph often were.

"Morning, Raoul," I said politely to one of the newer working students as I pushed past him with my wheelbarrow full of fragrant hay.

"There is nothing good about this morning," he muttered under his breath. "It's cold, dark, and there's still a week until payday. Not that that's anything much to look forward to. There's nothing to spend money on in this pitiful town anyway."

"Okay then," I said, hurrying past.

Raoul was a recent import from Portugal who'd been brought in to help Christoph start some of the younger horses under saddle. He was the same age as me and had enviously high cheekbones and thick dark lashes that made his huge brown eyes look bigger than they were. He had dark, wavy hair t and a sultry mouth that was too often curled into a lazy sneer.

He would have been strikingly beautiful if he was at all a nice person. But he wasn't. He could be charming when he wanted, but most of the time he sulked, complained and made nasty comments to the other grooms. If we hadn't been so short-staffed, I was sure Christoph would have sent him home long before now.

Raoul didn't have a chance to treat the horses badly under the watchful eye of Christoph, but he didn't seem to have any love or sympathy for them either. He didn't praise them or go out of his way to make friends, pet them or offer treats. To him they were just a job, machines that should be obedient no matter what they were feeling.

It was too bad, because technically he was a beautiful rider. But even though he had a picture-perfect position in the saddle, he'd never make it as a top-level rider and trainer if he didn't learn some empathy for the horses. So much of riding was about the relationship between rider and mount. At least for me, anyway.

I pushed my wheelbarrow down the long aisle, stepping aside suddenly for Sonja, who barged past me at a near-run carrying a stack of hay that towered high over her head. She always went everywhere at a brisk trot and seemed in a hurry all the time. But maybe that's because she had so much work to do.

"Hey, Jilly." Christoph, our head trainer, appeared in the office doorway. He was immaculately dressed in his usual uniform of tan breeches, brown leather riding boots, a tweed jacket and a matching tweed cap. His neatly trimmed mustache finished off the look of a retired English gentleman. "I was hoping to catch you first thing. We need to discuss when you will resume your riding duties. These horses need to be in full work; they can't sit around being idle forever."

"Oh … um," I said, caught off guard. Then I remembered that I had an actual excuse to not have this discussion right then. "Sorry, I can't. I have a job interview to go to right after chores. Maybe I'll catch up with you later."

"Job interview? How are you supposed to have a job and take care of your horses?"

"I know it won't be easy," I said, cutting off the rest of his lecture. "But this is something I have to do."

I dropped my voice and glanced around to make sure none of the grooms were nearby.

"I'm out of money, Christoph. I can't go on like this. I can't be a servant in my mother's house forever."

His face softened and he laid a hand on my shoulder.

"I support you no matter what, Jilly. But don't give up on the horses. You're so talented."

"Okay, thanks," I murmured, ducking past him before he could say more.

I made my way down the aisle to Bally's stall first and slipped inside to where the big horse was already waiting, his coat slightly translucent under the soft barn lights.

"There you go, big guy," I whispered to him and he whickered happily under his breath, burying his nose in the fragrant hay.

Behind me, I could feel the other grooms sending me sidelong glances. Someone nearby, probably Bethany, snickered under their breath and I took a deep breath to stay calm.

I didn't look up as I came out of Bally's stall and moved into Lark's.

One by one I fed my crew, then cleaned their stalls and topped up their bedding. There were never quite enough wheelbarrows to go around so I liked to get this part of my chore list done right away.

"Are you done with this?" Nick asked quietly as I dumped the last bag of shavings in Lark's stall. He didn't meet my eye, just pointed at my empty wheelbarrow. He was an ex-jockey who stood a few inches shy of five feet and normally he barely said a word.

"Sure, all yours," I said and he grabbed the handles and scuttled away.

As soon as the stalls were done, I went to the horses one by one to pull their heavy coats off before giving each animal a quick brush and putting on their lighter day blankets. All the horses besides my shaggy little colt Damascus, and ghostly Bally, had had their hair clipped short and their manes and tails neatly pulled so that they were ready to show or sell at a moment's notice. They looked beautiful, but it wasn't a very practical choice for icy February weather in Canada, so they were forced to wear an assortment of coats full time so they didn't freeze into popsicles.

"Is it okay if I quickly use the computer in here?" I asked Christoph who was just headed out of the office.

"Of course," he said, laying a kindly hand on my shoulder as he passed, "whatever you need. And you know, Jilly, if you ever want to talk to anyone … about anything at all. I'm always here."

"I know, thank you," I said, heading to the desk. Christoph's worry over me was growing day by day and if there was any way I could have relieved his mind without revealing my ghostly secret I would have.

The computer whirred to life and I waited impatiently to pull up my e-mail, eager to know if there was any word from my cousin Xan and his girlfriend Estelle at Dark Lady Farm.

I had my tablet back at the house but, like most modern technology, it didn't work very well inside the manor. I'd always thought that Mother had been against technology on principle; I'd never been allowed a television or to play computer games growing up. But it turned out that it was just the nature of Greystone. Something in the way it was built or the place it sat just shorted out most equipment brought into the house.

The kitchen appliances worked all right, and the washer and dryer seemed to run fine, but anything else just died within a few days or didn't work at all. I went through at least two phones a year and even then, the reception was hit or miss; phone calls were often garbled and my texts sometimes didn't arrive at their destination until hours, or days, later. If at all.

Finally, the page loaded and I read my new messages eagerly. Xan was an entertaining storyteller and he kept me smiling with his updates of the farm and his ongoing feud with old Jacob, my Great Aunt Ruth's cranky new husband. I think Xan guessed how lonely I was all by myself at Greystone and felt it was his duty to keep me in good spirits. He sent me a quick email nearly every day and told me about the horses he was training.

Twenty minutes later, I said goodbye to my horses and headed back to the house.

I peeled my snowy boots off by the kitchen door and went to stand in my sock feet on the blissfully warm tiles in front of the fire. No matter how insulated my boots were supposed to be, my toes were always numb by the time morning chores were over. My skin tingled as I began to thaw, and my mouth watered at the smell of the small pan of bacon sizzling on the stovetop.

"Oh, child, you're chilled right through." Betty swept into the kitchen holding a wooden serving tray full of clean, folded tea-towels from the laundry. She'd been with my family since before I was born so she still treated me like I was five years old even though I was a grown adult. "You should let me get you some hot coffee and breakfast, just this once."

I was sorely tempted, especially since she was the best cook in the world. Mother's orders to the few remaining staff had been to let me fend for myself. She'd meant it as a punishment since the idea of doing her own laundry probably gave her nightmares, but I'd relished in my sudden freedom and independence after a lifetime of being managed by servants.

"I'm all right, thanks, Betty. I'll just run upstairs and have a shower and then make something myself. But thanks for offering."

Resolutely ignoring the smell of freshly ground coffee wafting after me, I fled upstairs to have a steaming hot shower and get dressed into something suitable for an interview.

When I finally emerged from my walk-in closet wearing dark, dressy jeans and a button-down shirt, the rocking chair by the fire began to sway slowly back and forth of its own accord.

"Glad you approve, Nanny," I said, sending a smile in that general direction. "I was going for casual chic."

The chair rocked a few more times and then went still, which was a good sign. Nanny was my actual childhood nanny who'd been sent away when I was a teenager. She'd appeared to me again as a ghost on the night Bally died, the night my partially damaged gift came back. Although I could often sense spirits nearby, the *seeing* part was still a bit hit and miss. Sometimes I saw Nanny clear as day and sometimes I could just feel when she was around.

Nanny had come up with the theory that my gift was somehow linked to Bally's presence. When he was nearby, I could see her clearly, but the further he went from me the fainter she got.

"I think he acts as a conduit for you," Nanny had told me, "He strengthens your connection to the other side."

It was a good theory and so far, it seemed to be accurate. Still, even without his assistance, Nanny could let me know she was there in other ways. If her old chair rocked gently, it meant she was pleased, and any sort of agitated rocking meant I was in for a lecture once I could see and hear her again.

With my hair pulled back into a tidy ponytail and a trace

of makeup on my face, I was ready for breakfast. I looked at the clock and felt a surge of adrenaline; if I didn't get a move on, I'd be late.

I hurried out into the wide stone hallway, knocking against one of the free-standing display cases in my haste.

"Ow," I said, rubbing my smarting elbow and glaring down at the case, annoyed. We had them all over the house in the most inconvenient spots; square wooden bases with raised glass tops to protect whichever precious family heirloom lay inside on velvet cloths. Little cards listed the name of each item and there was a short description below. Like we were a bloody museum or something.

I stared down at the Serpent's Blade in distaste. It was one of my least-favoured objects. It was a finely wrought silver knife with a carved jade serpent coiled around it from hilt to pommel. Polished red carnelian eyes stared back unblinkingly and I suppressed a shiver. I'd never liked that knife. It was sharp enough on its own to kill, but it also contained a deadly secret. A thin groove ran from handle to tip and ended in a compartment in the snake's mouth that could be used to store a small amount of poison. When released, the poison would run inside the groove down to the tip. Depending on the poison, it could take just one tiny knife cut to kill someone.

My skin prickled and I felt a shivery touch on the back of my neck, just for a moment. I rubbed my arms to whisk the goosebumps away and ran the rest of the way downstairs.

"You have to have something more than toast," Betty scolded as I bit into a slice of her delicious homemade bread slathered with peanut butter.

"I don't have time this morning," I said hastily, finishing my toast and coffee at warp speed. "I'm already running behind. I have to make sure that beast of a car starts, too."

Myrtle, as I'd christened her, was an ancient purple Volkswagen Beetle that I'd hastily purchased from one of the departing grooms when he'd quit.

After a week of slaving away in the barn, he'd announced that he was quitting riding for good and selling everything so he could buy a one-way ticket to New York City to work in theater.

I probably should have asked more questions but the price was right. I bought her without doing any of the usual things like having a vehicle inspection or, say, asking the opinion of anyone who knew about cars. Mr. Hopps, the ancient old chauffeur who took care of my parent's car collection, had been appalled and refused point-blank to have anything to do with her. He wouldn't even let Myrtle stay in the garage with her fancier cousins. I had to keep her out in a shed behind the stables.

I wasn't the boldest of drivers at the best of times, but Myrtle's quirks had driven me to jaw-clenching terror more than once. She also didn't like to start sometimes when the weather was too cold, or too damp, or too hot. Mr. Hopps had finally taken pity on me and installed a block heater so I could at least plug her in during the worst of winter.

Now, fully coated and booted again, I trekked back out through the drifts and threw open the doors to the little shed where Myrtle sat sulkily in the darkness. It was an old storage shed that had piles of dusty boxes at one end and rafters full of cobwebs.

"Hello, old girl," I said encouragingly, unplugging her cord and stuffing it back under the grill. I tossed my satchel full of résumés into the passenger side and slid onto the cold, cracked leather driver's seat. I put the key into the ignition and, holding my breath, gave it a turn.

The car choked a few times, puffing smoke, and then grumbled to life. Silently cheering to the car gods, I eased her out into the snow. Myrtle didn't have four-wheel drive but she did have front-wheel traction, which ate up even the deep snow in a steady, determined way. I stopped and let the engine idle while I got back out to shut the shed door. If I didn't, Myrtle's make-shift garage would be full of drifts by the time I got back and I'd have to shovel it out again; I'd learned that lesson the hard way.

I swung the first half of the door into place but just as I reached for the second half it jerked out of my hand and shut itself with a bang.

I bit back a yelp of surprise and nearly fell on my backside in the snow. This had been happening more and more frequently over the last few months as my gift grew stronger; invisible hands moving things around or knocking things over. I was still learning, but I'd discovered that there was a certain feeling in the air when a particular unseen ghost was around. Bally's presence made me think of sweet hay and peaceful green fields, and when Nanny was around it was all cozy warm fires and hot chocolate. This spirit had a sort of deep woodsy essence to it that I couldn't quite place. I didn't think I needed to be frightened of it, but it also seemed a little testy. When it was feeling particularly feisty it would thump the dusty boxes around like it was playing the drums.

"Um, thank you," I said into the empty air. A leafless tree beside the shed shivered and dropped a load of snow to the ground with a thud and I decided that it was time to go.

## Chapter 3

There wasn't any traffic on an early Saturday morning and Myrtle handled the steep, icy hill down into Maplegrove better than I'd expected. I only skidded twice in the corners, bouncing gently off the high banks of snow that lined the road. I was travelling slowly enough, and Myrtle was solid enough, that this was a pretty effective way of steering. We made it into town without any major incidents.

The roads right in town had been plowed so I was able to park directly across the street from MapleBrew. I found a spot in front of Curiosity, the local bookstore and turned the ignition off in relief. I'd made it.

I looked at the small gold watch I'd strapped to my wrist for the occasion; there were still ten minutes to spare before my very first interview. I took a deep breath to compose my jangling nerves.

I'd spent hours preparing for this; I'd studied all sorts of articles on résumé-building and the art of being a good interviewee. I'd practiced my interview skills so many times in front of Betty that she was heartily sick of me. Even Bally and

Nanny had started avoiding me when I brought out my meagre résumé for yet another round of edits.

I'd never had a job in my life besides showing horses so this was a big deal for me. I had a car, a colt and a cat to pay for now, and it was time to take responsibility for my future.

"Right," I said to my reflection in the rear-view mirror. "Let's do this."

Myrtle's rusty door squealed loudly in protest when I pried it open and again when I slammed it shut. A large chunk of rust fell from her rear passenger door and embedded itself in a snow drift. Two teenaged boys who were huddled under the bookstore awning burst out laughing.

"Nice ride, lady," the taller one joked. I ignored them, marching resolutely across the road to MapleBrew.

*Home to the World's Best Cinnamon Buns*, the signboard outside proudly proclaimed, and I had to agree. They had four different types including maple drizzle, peanut butter, cream cheese, and apple. I was a sucker for the peanut butter.

The delicious smell hit me the second I opened the door and I inhaled gratefully, feeling a shiver of delight at the anticipation of working in a pleasant place like this. The café was packed with customers starting their day with coffee and a treat.

"Hello, Jilly. I'll be right with you." The young barista, Katie, smiled from behind the counter and waved me to an unoccupied table in the corner. She was an older high school student who worked at the café evenings and weekends. She'd been the one to encourage me to drop off my résumé in the first place and she'd set up the interview for me with her boss.

I watched enviously as she whipped up a series of complicated-looking coffees for the two women waiting at the counter. She seemed to master the big machine effortlessly, pushing buttons that made things froth and foam and blend to her will.

She never stopped moving and I secretly wondered if I'd ever be able to keep up a pace like that, let alone work the machine.

I didn't have long to think about it though because an icy blast of air from the door made me look up. I winced when I found my old nemesis Kristal Saunders staring down at me with a condescending look on her face. Her platinum-blonde hair hung past her shoulders and she had on a red Burberry coat and matching boots that made her look exceptionally pretty and equally intimidating.

She added a raised eyebrow and the signature sneer she'd used on me since public school, and despite being well out of high school, I gulped nervously in response. I hadn't had anything to do with her since we'd graduated but apparently, she'd kept her hatred for me burning strong.

"Hi, Aunt Kristal," Katie called from the counter, completely oblivious to the small drama playing out over here, "that's your interview, Jillian, I'll be right over as soon as I'm done here."

*Aunt* Kristal? My heart sank. How had I not known she was Katie's aunt? If Kristal was MapleBrew's manager then I was toast. What had happened to the nice older lady who'd run it before?

"No need," Kristal said, magnifying her voice so everyone in a two-block radius could hear. "I don't think it will work out. Sorry for wasting your time, Jillian, but ... you're just not the *type* of person we're looking for."

She sent me a deadly smile, folding her arms across her chest. She glanced triumphantly around the café as if expecting her patrons to leap up and break into a round of applause.

"But why?" Katie asked in confusion, looking almost as upset as I felt. "We need someone and she'd be perfect. No one else has even applied yet. I'm working overtime as it is."

Before Kristal could start listing off all my faults, I stood up abruptly, my cheeks burning with mortification. "Thanks for considering me," I blurted and then fled the warmth of the shop onto the wintery street outside.

Tears stung my eyes as I half-ran across the road toward the safety of my car, trying to squash the hurt and anger Krystal had triggered in me.

Ever since kindergarten she'd had it out for me. When we were little, she'd pushed and tripped and called me names. As a teenager, she'd used subtler, but equally cruel, tactics. Now, as an adult, it looked like she planned to keep the tradition alive.

I was too distracted to see the icy patch in front of me until I'd stepped directly in the middle of it and went down like a ton of bricks, my arms wind-milling in the air like something out of a cartoon. I hit the ground hard, my elbow thwacking the pavement and I yelped in pain and surprise. My satchel flew into the snowbank beside me, clasps exploding outward. My carefully prepared résumés flew out and fluttered into the street.

Laughter filled the air and I looked up in outrage to see the same teenaged boys as before standing under the bookstore awning howling with glee. Well, one was howling, the other laughed nervously and looked away in embarrassment when I met his gaze.

"I give it an eight," the taller, dark-haired one shouted. "She loses points for form but gains some for creativity. That was priceless."

"Right," the second boy said doubtfully, "that's pretty funny."

I winced as I struggled to sit up. My elbow and knee hurt where I'd hit the ground and I could feel my cheeks burning. The bookstore was right across from MapleBrew's huge front window; there was no way anyone would have missed my stellar performance.

The dark-haired boy looked down at me with no mercy

and no sympathy. He was still laughing but there was a cruel glint of excitement in his eyes like a predator closing in for a kill. For a second, I didn't see him as a teenager, I only saw waves of oily darkness roiling inside of him.

The shame from my fall and my failed interview gave way to a new emotion; anger.

I wasn't used to feeling rage. The procedure that had suppressed my gifts as a teenager had also squashed down my stronger emotions. I'd become adept at avoiding conflict in order to get along.

But now the guard on my temper was gone and I felt fury flowing through my veins like lava. At the same time, an icy wind shot down the street toward me, swirling snow in all directions like a miniature hurricane. I clenched my fists and the wind grew even stronger.

The bell over Curiosity's door rang sharply, startling me out of my anger. The wind died, the snow settled and I took a deep breath.

There were a couple of sharp yelps of surprise, and then both the boys brushed past me at a run, nearly knocking me over again as they went past.

"Toby, you get back here," an elderly voice called, "you're still grounded. Your father told you to stay here until he picks you up."

"Sorry, Mr. G. I'm going to Sam's house."

"Yeah, lay off old man," the taller boy called, "he's busy."

He shot another smug glance at me over his shoulder, curling his lip in a snarl.

*What horrible boys*, I thought, staring after them as they ran down the icy sidewalk and around the corner.

"Are you hurt, child?" a kind, wavery voice asked.

I looked up to see old, white-haired Mr. Galinski tottering

toward me across the slick sidewalk, his eyes flickering anxiously between me and the spot where the boys had disappeared.

"Oh, thank you, I'm fine," I said, pushing myself carefully to my feet. I picked my satchel up, stuffing in the few scattered résumés that hadn't been blown away. "Just my pride is bruised."

"Well, I'm sorry you had to be subjected to such rude behaviour. Toby is a good boy at heart, a smart boy, but he persists in running around with the wrong crowd wherever he goes. I'm afraid he will come to a bad end if he doesn't start thinking for himself soon."

"Oh," I said, surprised at his vehemence.

"Forgive me, here I am leaving you standing in the snow when you obviously need a cup of tea and some quiet conversation."

"Thank you," I said politely, "that's very kind. But I should get going. I need to track down those résumés before they're spread all over town."

I looked around, knowing that it was already too late. They were probably all miles away by now.

"Résumés?" he said, looking interested. "Are you looking for a job?"

"Well, yes I …"

"I don't suppose you like to read, do you?"

"I do, actually," I said with a smile. Reading and horses were the things I liked best in the world. If I could find a way to combine the two and do them at the same time I probably would.

"Excellent, excellent, well, come inside and get warm, Jillian Harrington. We'll do our interview by the fire. I find myself in sudden need of an assistant."

Bewildered that he even knew my name and by this sudden turn of events, I followed him into the bookstore. The bell chimed cheerfully behind me as the door closed, shutting out the cold.

"Amazing," I breathed, looking around in wonder. I hadn't been in here since high school. Mr. Galinski had always seemed a little scary to me when I was younger and I'd taken to avoiding town altogether in recent years. Ever since my disastrous engagement party where my awful ex-fiancé, Frederick, had dumped me in front of the entire town.

Curiosity was one of the few shops in town that my parents didn't own. Which was amazing since they had pretty much bought up everything else.

Mother had a great instinct for sensing when people were hurting for cash and feeling desperate. She knew just when to swoop in and make a painfully low offer they couldn't refuse. Then, to sweeten the deal she'd often rent their stores back to them at a premium.

There was a lot of anger and resentment against my family in this town.

The shop was bigger than I remembered. A tall, polished wooden counter stood just inside the door, topped with an old cash register that had probably been new sometime in the 1800s. The floor was dark, polished wood with brocade runner carpets laid down just inside the door by the till where customers could get the worst of the snow off their boots. The floorboards creaked underfoot as I walked, making me feel like I'd been transported back in time a hundred years or so.

The rest of the store had been completely given over to hundreds of shelves of neatly stacked books. They lined the walls around the perimeter of the room and then enormous free-standing shelves took over the whole middle part. They stood in four precise rows like oversized dominoes leaving a wide aisle to walk down the middle between them.

"How about you look around while I get the tea ready,"

Mr. Galinski said, giving me a gentle push toward the stacks. I didn't need to be told twice.

I walked around in a happy daze, running my fingers along the leather and paper spines, quickly learning the layout of the store. The left side was given over to non-fiction and the right side, along with a cozy back alcove I discovered, were devoted to fiction. There was another room off to the left that had a shut door with a gold plaque that read *Rare Books Collection* neatly engraved on it. I tried the handle out of curiosity but it was locked. Down a short hall that was lined with more books, there was a little kitchen and bathroom area and then at the very end, there was an office with a desk that must have been where Mr. Galinski did his paperwork. I didn't want to intrude so I doubled back to the little alcove.

The cozy space was a perfect reading nook. A fire crackled merrily in the hearth and around it was a set of well-worn leather couches with matching footstools so guests could put their feet up and read in peace. The wooden end tables that flanked each couch were stacked with even more books. There was a narrow door off to one side with a little brass plaque that read *Private Residence* on it and I remembered that Mr. Galinski lived in a flat above the shop.

There was a little tea station in the corner of the alcove where guests could help themselves to a hot drink and biscuits while they read.

Empty cups and a plate sprinkled with cookie crumbs sat on one of the end tables by the couch, and I automatically scooped them up and sat them on a trolley in the corner that had a little card on it with the words *please put dirty dishes here* written in scrolling handwriting.

"Excellent," Mr. Galinski said, beaming at me as he tottered into the room. "I'm afraid most people never pass the first test so easily."

"Test?" I asked in confusion.

"Oh nothing, nothing, just the whims of a fussy old man. You put the dirty dishes away, you see, not many do. It shows that you have a tidy mind."

"Hmm," I said, wondering what he'd say if he could see the very-untidy contents of my tumultuous mind, "well, thank you."

"Jillian Harrington, I find myself much in need of an assistant. You see, my godson Toby was sent here by his father Professor Mason, who is a dear old colleague. It was to see if living away from the big city would help the boy sort out his wild streak. I'm afraid that the experiment has not been a success. I recently caught him attempting to steal a very important document from the rare books collection, although what he planned to do with it, I can't say. I've had no choice but to decide to let him go and send him back to his father."

"Oh, I'm sorry. He looks so young though. Shouldn't he be in school?"

"Yes, he should be." Mr. Galinski sighed, looking troubled. "He was kicked out of his last school for stealing as well. I don't believe that he's a wicked boy by nature. He's bright, inquisitive, and loves to read. At first, I thought he was fitting in perfectly. He'd made nice friends in the neighbourhood and he worked hard in the shop. But then he started to act differently, and he fell in with the wrong crowd here. He is not strong of character and is easily influenced by others, I'm afraid. Now, Toby's father is determined to send him to military school to straighten him out. It's a bad business all around."

"I'm sorry," I said again, not knowing what else to say.

He clapped his hands together and shook his head. "No matter, I won't take up the rest of your day with my troubles, Miss. Harrington, let's talk books."

The next hour was spent sipping delicious tea and telling Mr. Galinski why the books that I loved the most were my favourites. He wanted to know what parts I liked best and what sort of lessons I'd learned from them. He wanted to know about themes and contexts and plot lines. I hadn't been asked questions like those since high school, I just read for pleasure now, but the questions made those unused parts of my brain slowly wake up and begin to think again. Soon I warmed up to the discussion and was happily chattering away to him.

There was only one strange moment that gave me pause and made me wonder if perhaps Mr. Galinski wasn't feeling his age a little.

He'd stopped suddenly in mid-sentence and held up a finger, tilting his head to one side as if he were listening.

"Did you hear that?" he asked in a whisper.

I listened but heard nothing but a faint, steady ticking sound from somewhere deep in the shop, perhaps a clock counting down the time.

A floorboard creaked behind us and we both turned toward the sound. There was nothing there. But that wasn't surprising, creaking floorboards were commonplace in an old building like this. Greystone's floors cracked and popped all the time.

After a minute, Mr. Galinski shrugged and shook his head. "I must be getting old," he said and then went back to talking about books as if nothing had happened.

He didn't ask me anything practical like whether I knew how to use the ancient cash register or if I had any experience in sales but by the end of our discussion he was satisfied.

"You will start tomorrow morning at nine o clock, sharp," he said happily. And that was that. I had landed my very first job.

I practically skipped out of the store and narrowly missed falling for a second time that day when Katie popped out in front of me right next to my car.

"Ack," I yelped, skidding to a stop just in time.

"Sorry," she said breathlessly. "I saw you go inside earlier and I've been standing out here forever in the cold waiting for you to leave."

"You look half-frozen. Why were you waiting?"

"I wanted to apologize for Aunt Kristal. I don't know what came over her. I think you would have been perfect for the café."

"Oh, don't worry," I said quickly, "Mr. Galinski just hired me to help in the bookstore so it worked out perfectly. Kristal and I have been fighting since kindergarten. I didn't know she managed MapleBrew or I wouldn't have applied."

"She bought the café from Mrs. Wright this winter but she's been managing it for a while now." Katie looked down and bit her lip. "That's great Mr. G hired you. He's the best. I used to come over and hang out with Toby before ..."

"Before what?"

Katie looked down and bit her lip. "It doesn't matter. I just used to hang out there, that's all. Anyway, I know that Kristal comes across as a... well, as not very nice sometimes but she has a great heart. She helped my mom out and gave me a job when she hardly even knew me. She can be really fun, too."

"I didn't know she had a sister. Did we go to school together?"

"No." She shook her head. "They're half-sisters and my mom was raised in the city by her grandparents. Kristal didn't know much about us until recently. I'm sorry that we won't be working together. I've wanted to get to know you properly ever since my mom and I moved here."

"Me?" I said in astonishment. "Why?"

"Because you have all those amazing horses. I used to ride before we had to move. I've even seen you at some of the bigger shows. I loved your grey horse Ballymore, and I was so sorry to hear that he died. I cried when I read it online."

"Um, thanks," I said, feeling that sharp stab to the gut I always felt when I was caught off guard by someone mentioning him. Even though Bally was with me in his ghostly form, his death still hit me hard.

Katie looked down too and kicked at a chunk of snow.

"Do you give lessons?" she asked suddenly.

"No." I shook my head and then winced when her hopeful expression fell. "I mean, I've never given lessons before."

"Oh, well, that's all right." Katie sighed and looked back toward the café. "Maybe I could just come up to Greystone and meet the horses sometime. We've been here almost a year and I haven't even *seen* a horse let alone ridden one."

"Did you ride lots where you lived before?"

"Yes, two or three times a week if I could. And I helped exercise the client's horses when they didn't have time. I worked at the barn on weekends and after school, cleaning stalls or feeding or whatever they wanted in exchange for lessons."

"Did you ever show?" I asked thoughtfully, an idea suddenly taking root in my brain.

"A little. I mostly groomed for the other riders, but sometimes I showed one of the school horses, too."

"All right, what's your number?" I asked pulling out my phone. My contact list was painfully short and I felt a bit proud as I added in a new number. "I'll call you and you can come up after work one night and meet the horses."

"Really? Oh, thank you." Katie was all smiles now. "I'd better get back to work but thank you again."

I walked back to my car feeling immensely satisfied with my morning. It was so strange how things had worked out. Yeah, the episode at MapleBrew had been mortifying. But the bookstore was a much better fit for me. And I'd unexpectedly managed to make a new horsey friend. Things were looking up.

Myrtle started instantly, which was another miracle, and I shot off toward home to tell my ghosts the good news.

## Chapter 4

*T*here was no sign of Bally or Nanny when I got home. Even Betty was missing in action. She'd been spending an awful lot of time in town doing volunteer work lately, ever since my parents and their entourage had left. We were used to the house being filled with people and I wondered if she felt as lonely as I did lately. Unlike Betty, I was used to spending time alone. And lately, I had been steadily working my way through about ten years' worth of repressed trauma, re-discovering ghosts and trying to figure out what I wanted from life. So, I probably hadn't been the best company for her.

I made myself a sandwich and left her a note in the kitchen, letting her know that I'd gotten a job.

*I should text Gil too,* I thought. *He's the one always pushing me to be independent of this crazy family. He'll be thrilled.*

My relationship with Gil was complicated to say the least. But he was still the person I loved best in the world, aside from Bally, and he'd been encouraging me to get away from Greystone since we were about eight years old. We'd always planned to run away and start our own stable together but things hadn't quite worked out that way. At least not yet.

I sent him a quick message, knowing that with our sketchy cell service it might be days before he got it, and then carried my sandwich and a cup of coffee to the big library.

I sighed a little as I looked around, not taking as much pleasure as I usually did from being surrounded by books. After my pleasant morning in town with Mr. Galinski, the beautiful library seemed even emptier than usual.

There was an old leather-bound book on the table in front of me and I picked it up reluctantly, searching for the page I'd left off on. The cover felt slick against my fingers and I had to force myself not to put it down.

This particular book was a family history that had been written by one of my ancestors—an angry, bitter old tyrant named Alocious. He had made it his life's mission to document and study the peculiar genetic gifts our family possessed.

He also had been a greedy, miserly old man who only viewed the gifts as something to be used to make his vast fortune even bigger. He'd despised women and had thought them incapable of managing their power without the help of fathers and husbands.

He believed that the gifts that could make our family money were divinely ordained while less useful powers were evil. Something that needed to be stamped out. According to him, my gift of ghosts fell into the second category.

Even though I didn't like my ancestor at all, I felt it was important to read the book; it helped me to understand the forces that had shaped our family and also be prepared for what gifts I might encounter in others were. Cousin Alastair and Aimee had had access to multiple gifts; bending fire, magical potions, mind control…. Something I was still trying to wrap my head around.

It wasn't likely that members of our crazy family would ever try and attack me again. But it was best to be prepared just in case.

Alocious had also been known for perfecting the art of removing, or attempting to remove, undesirable gifts from his descendants, especially the girls of the family. It was thought that removing one gift would make way for more lucrative abilities, but it didn't always work out that way.

Mother willingly sacrificed her gift when she was a teenager, and in her case, she had developed powerful precognition in its place. It hadn't worked that way for my Great Aunt Ruth and it hadn't worked that way for me either. Ruth had spent most of her life in lonely, bitter resentment and I had very nearly followed in her footsteps. I was lucky that what was left of my damaged gift had come back at all.

A chill passed over my arm, and I flinched and looked up. A faint smell of lavender washed over me and the pages of Alocious's book fluttered a little under my fingers. A second later, the book snapped shut on its own and then it shot down to the end of the table.

"Hello, library ghost," I said, putting a hand protectively over my sandwich before she whisked it away too. "Sorry, I know you hate that book. I kind of do too. But it needs to be read."

I hadn't *seen* this ghost yet but she'd been making herself known for months and I'd gotten a good idea of her personality. She was partly helpful and partly an obsessive-compulsive cleaner who couldn't stand any sort of disorder.

She was good at finding the titles I was looking for. I would often just have to say the names out loud and they'd either fall off a shelf at my feet or end up on my desk.

But she didn't like books being left out, or crumbs on the table. And she didn't like me reading Alocious's book.

Unfortunately, I didn't know the history of everyone who'd worked or lived at Greystone so I had no idea if she was a relative of mine or someone who'd been employed there. Or maybe she was a random ghost who'd wandered in off the street.

"Just let me finish my sandwich and I'll be out of your hair for the rest of the day," I promised her.

The lavender smell grew stronger and then the pile of hand-written papers to my right began to flutter. I glanced over and pulled the sheets slowly toward me.

I'd been working on a bit of a mystery since I'd come home to Greystone and I'd hit a road block that I couldn't seem to get around.

I'd lost most of my memories of the summer my gift had been taken away. Because that's what happened when creepy doctors poked around in your brain without permission.

But one fragment had come back to me when I'd been at Dark Lady. Just an image of me, standing in the pouring rain holding an armful of notebooks. The feeling that went with that image was one of desperation and fear.

Gil had told me that I'd written in notebooks all the time when I was a kid and a teenager. That I'd journaled non-stop and written down all sorts of ideas and inventions and stories about the ghosts of Greystone.

He thought they'd just been stories of course but I knew now that they were real.

The journals had disappeared right around the same time as my memories had and Gil had a theory that I'd hidden the notebooks somewhere on the property without telling anyone. Somewhere my mother would never think to look.

There was a possibility that she'd destroyed them all a long time ago of course. When I'd confronted her, she had insisted that she had no idea what notebooks I was talking about.

But, if there was a chance that younger me had hidden them somewhere then I had to find them. That's what all the notes were about. I'd listed off all the places I'd liked to go as a kid and then had started exploring them and crossing them off one by one.

Of course, there were a million places. I'd been an adventurous kid and Greystone was a big property. I could probably look for years without finding them.

The papers fluttered again and I frowned in confusion.

"Are you mad because I left these out?" I asked. "Or are you trying to tell me something? If you know where the notebooks are I'd love some help."

But there was no answer. The smell of lavender died away and the breeze stopped as quickly as it had started.

Far down the hall, I could hear Mrs. Hopps and her helpers doing their weekly deep cleaning of the manor. Every Saturday they worked over Greystone from top to bottom, even though most of the rooms now stood empty, noisily giving everything a good scrub.

The Dutch (or was it Swiss?), girls kept up a constant conversation in another language, laughing at their own jokes and obviously having a good time. Mrs. Hopps just worked in grim silence.

When they reached the library and she caught sight of me, Mrs. Hopps sighed noisily and looked at my nearly empty plate and cup mournfully, as if I'd left her a colossal mess to clean up.

"Don't hurry on our account," Mrs. Hopps said dolefully as she and the Dutch girls set their buckets of cleaning supplies down with a series of clatters and stared at me. "Take your time. We'll just wait."

I took the hint and stood up, stuffing the last of my sandwich into my mouth and gathering up my plate and coffee cup to take to the kitchen. The Dutch girls giggled nervously as I passed and Mrs. Hopps sent them an irritated glare.

It was time to exercise the horses anyway. They needed to stretch their legs no matter what the weather was like or they'd go stir-crazy cooped up in their stalls. Not having proper winter turnout was the only downside to Greystone. The horses were full of pent-up energy when the weather was bad.

Because I still didn't ride yet, my horses had to be hand-walked around the big indoor arena to warm up and then carefully lunged at the end of a long cotton line in circles, working at a walk, trot, and then a canter to loosen their muscles and get their blood flowing again.

Then, when they'd worn the most of their energy off, I worked them in-hand with their bridles on to develop their suppleness and relaxation.

Damascus, the colt who'd been my parting gift from Great Aunt Ruth, was a baby so his routine was a little different, and he was by far the easiest to work with. I treated him the same way I'd treated Bally back when he was alive; I just unclipped his lead and let him tear around the ring like a wild thing, bucking and leaping and pretending to scare himself until he'd worn off that first layer of energy.

Once he was able to focus on me, I just played with him, asking him to move up to a trot and canter and down to a walk again using my voice and body language. I asked him to change directions a few times and then called him in and gave him his carrot and told him what a good boy he was. After that, we worked on whichever trick I was teaching him at the moment. Right now, it was getting him to bow, but he wasn't quite as bright a student as Bally had been at that age so it was taking a while for him to get the concept. He could touch his nose to his knee, and he could put his front foot out in the bow position, but he hadn't figured out how to put the two together. Still, I gave him praise and treats for the slightest attempt and made sure that he thought himself quite clever.

I would have much rather treated all the horses this way, but they belonged to Greystone, not me, and they were an expensive investment. There was always the slim chance that they'd injure themselves playing too hard and ruin their careers. I was willing to risk it, but they were Mother's property, not mine, so I obediently followed the program even though these days it frustrated both me and the horses to tears.

Serena, Lark, and Lilo went through their routine obediently enough; they didn't care what they did as long as they were out getting exercise. Allison, on the other hand, showed her displeasure by being as naughty as possible both in hand and on the lunge line. She nipped at my fingers and tried to crowd me and step on my feet. And on the lunge line, she broke into a gallop whenever she felt like it, half-dragging me across the ring.

"I'd probably be safer riding you than lunging you," I muttered as I led her back to her stall. I hadn't been working with Allison long before Bally and I had been shot, but I remembered that she'd been a fun horse to ride, very bold and full of power. But that she'd been challenging when things weren't going her way.

"You need to get outside to wear off some of that energy, don't you?" I asked, petting her damp neck.

"What she *needs* is a rider," Christoph said as I walked the big mare past him toward the wash stall, her hooves clopping loudly on the concrete aisle. "She's an athlete, not a backyard pony, Jilly, she can't be lunged forever. Maybe I could get Raoul to—"

"No," I said flatly. "Not him."

"Well, the other riders are too busy to take on more horses. They're all overworked as it is and foaling season is around the corner, and then we'll be more short-staffed than ever. Your horses are going down in value every day they sit idle. I don't know what you suggest. I can advertise for another working student, but it's not exactly easy to lure someone here in the dead of winter."

"I might have figured that out, actually," I said, remembering my conversation with Katie that morning. "It probably wouldn't work for Allison since she's so feisty, but I might have found someone who could ride the other horses."

"Hmm," he said skeptically, his mustache bristling. "What level is this person riding at?"

"I don't know. I just met her and I've never seen her ride. But she's local and she's shown a little."

"Bah," Christoph said, "we don't need another amateur. I don't have time for a student—"

"Well, I can teach her, can't I?" I interrupted, "Serena's easy enough to handle, we could start with her. And Lilo would be fine too. At least let's give the girl a chance."

"You want to teach her?" Christoph asked curiously, his bristly eyebrows rising in surprise.

"Sure, it would be a good winter project anyway. I can teach on my days off and after work."

And then I had to fill Christoph in on my new job, which he took with as much grace as he could manage. I knew he wanted me to work with the horses full time, but he was kind enough to at least pretend to be happy for me.

"It will be good to see you not moping around anymore," he said brusquely before striding away.

By that time, it was late in the afternoon. Working five horses didn't sound like much but the hours had faded away and my stomach was rumbling with hunger once again.

I lightly picked the stalls and made sure the horses still had hay to snack on before I trekked back to the house to take care of my grumbling stomach.

Betty might have resisted cooking especially for me under Mother's orders, but it didn't stop her from just happening to bake things and leave them around for me to find. This time it was a fragrant quiche cooling on the counter. My stomach growled in anticipation and I knew there was no way I could resist.

I piled a big slice on my plate and headed upstairs to see if Nanny and Bally were back from their ghostly errands yet. I still had to tell them all about my new job.

I was in luck.

"Oh, good for you, Jillian," Nanny said, looking up from her clacking knitting needles. She'd been working on the same red blanket since she'd first appeared to me in the fall and the project somehow never got any bigger. "Sid Galinski is just your type too, what with all the scientific experiments and things."

Bally snorted from where he'd been dozing next to the fire and pricked his ears toward my quiche, his nostrils twitching. He'd been like that even before he was a ghost. He would eat anything he could get his teeth on when we were at horse shows; mini donuts, burgers, chewing gum, leftover coffee. The worse it was for him, the more he wanted it.

"He's not a scientist, Nanny," I said patiently. Sometimes she got a little confused. "He runs the bookstore."

"I know what I know, Jillian Harrington, so don't you go acting like I'm senile yet."

"Of course not," I said hurriedly, "I don't know why I didn't think of applying there in the first place though, it's the perfect spot for me to work."

"And that Sid is not bad to look at, if I remember correctly," Nanny said, raising her eyebrows at me suggestively.

"What?" I choked on my food. "Ew, he's nearly a hundred, Nanny."

"Don't talk with your mouth full," she said sharply, "and don't sass your elders."

"Fine," I muttered.

Before she'd appeared to me as a ghost, I'd spent my whole life missing Nanny. I'd somehow forgotten over the years how bossy, feisty, and full of unsolicited advice she'd been. That was the way it was with family sometimes. You had to take the bad with the good.

"And what did young Gilbert say when you told him about your new job? He's always such a nice, polite boy, and so supportive," Nanny said, giving her chair a few extra vigorous rocks back and forth. Her concept of time could be a bit hazy; sometimes she knew that Gil and I were adults and sometimes she thought we were twelve again.

"Oh, I texted him but he hasn't gotten back to me. He's probably training hard there. I'm sure he's just busy."

"Nonsense. He's never been too busy for you. You should call him on the telephone. Or better still, bake him a pie and take it over to him. Boys like pie."

It took all my willpower to hold back my snort of laughter.

Nanny did not take kindly to being laughed at.

"It's not the 1950s, Nanny," I said once I'd mostly recovered. "And he's not here, remember? He's in Virginia with Coconut."

"I never did like coconuts," Nanny said, wrinkling her nose, "they smell like old socks if you ask me. Now, that boy has only been avoiding you because you're not being honest with him. He knows you're keeping secrets. He told you his worst secret and now you're holding out on telling him yours."

I stared at her in astonishment and swallowed hard. I'd forgotten how perceptive she could be at times.

"I know," I said slowly. "I should tell him about the ghost thing. You're right. But, Nanny. Do you remember what happened right before you were sent away from Greystone? Right before I lost my gift?"

"Er, well, there was a small near-drowning incident but…"

"I jumped into the river chasing down a ghost, Nanny. And Gil followed me. We both nearly died. *He* nearly died. And that was all my fault."

"Nonsense, Jillian you were a child."

"Yes, but honestly I knew more about ghosts then than I do now. And some of them can be dangerous. I remember that. If I make Gil part of this world then he's going to want to follow me around and try to protect me. I'll be putting him in the path of danger all the time. And I don't think I can risk that."

Nanny was silent for a long time. The only sound was her knitting needles clacking together.

"So, you're just going to make that decision for him? Without even giving him a chance to decide on his own?" She said finally. She didn't sound angry. She sounded sad.

For some reason, tears welled up in my eyes but I brushed them away impatiently.

"No, I'm not saying that. I haven't decided what I'm going to do yet. I just need more time to think about it. Maybe once I have more control of my gift then I'll feel better about telling him."

"Hmmm, maybe," Nanny said, but she didn't sound convinced. "Just don't wait too long. And have you considered making him a pie?"

Ah, we were back on familiar, safer ground.

"Thanks for the talk, Nanny," I said, getting to my feet. "I'll think about it."

I spent the rest of the day doing laundry, tidying my room, and combing my wardrobe for appropriate work clothes that hadn't spent time in the barn.

Mrs. Hopps did her usual grumbling when I used the washing machine but I ignored her. She always acted like I was going to use too much soap and blow it up or something. I wasn't a complete idiot.

Even though it was hardly past five o clock, the sky was darkening fast. This time of winter, you felt like you only got a taste of daylight before it was nighttime again. I was very much looking forward to Spring.

I fed everyone hay and then took turns brushing each one and hand-walking them around the arena a few times to stretch their legs. When they were cooped up in their stalls, all the horses had to get out for some sort of exercise at least twice a day. It made a heavier workload for all the barn staff, but we found that the horses stayed happier, healthier and less prone to injury with this program.

I did another trick-training session with Damascus, this time working on getting him to back up and move his hindquarters from one side to the other when I pointed at them. He'd picked this up very quickly and was justifiably proud of himself.

"Good job, buddy," I said, giving him a horse treat and a pat on the neck.

He crunched his cookie, arching his neck proudly at my praise. He'd blossomed over the last few months and his confidence had grown in leaps and bounds. He'd been a bit neglected back at Dark Lady Farm. He'd been an awkward and ungainly colt, and nobody had had very high hopes for him there. Nobody had thought much of him here either when I'd brought him back with me, but he'd filled out and was gaining muscle day by day. I'd even overheard two of the grooms praising him.

"He's going to be fancy. She sure has an eye for horses, even if she is crazy," I'd overheard Bethany saying to Dora a few weeks ago. They hadn't noticed that I was right behind them.

"She's not crazy," Dora had answered with a shrug, "just a little weird. She's better than her psycho mother anyway."

I guess that was some consolation.

After putting Damascus away, I picked out my stalls again and cleaned my tack. I finally had to admit that there was nothing else to do in the barn to keep myself occupied. I reluctantly headed back home.

The big house was quiet when I got back. Mrs. Hopps and the Dutch girls had gone home and Betty was already in bed. There was no sign of either Bally or Nanny, either. I made a small supper of baked beans on toast and ate in the big dining room all by myself, trying to get lost in a new novel.

It was a lonely dinner, brightened only by Morris jumping on the table and seating himself next to my plate, watching me eat with avid interest. It was an awful habit but I didn't discourage him; I'd never had my own house pet before, and I loved having him around for companionship. I never got bored watching his antics and, I may have been biased, but he seemed like an extra intelligent cat, almost like he understood what I was saying to him.

"Here you go," I said, pushing a small crust of bread with some sauce on it across the table toward him. I was heartily glad that nobody was around to see how much I spoiled him.

A cool, prickling feeling danced over my neck and I shivered. Morris looked up from his snack and stared balefully over my shoulder for a moment then gave a small hiss and jumped down from the table, the crust of bread still clamped between his teeth.

I sighed as the faint smell of lemon washed over me.

"Sorry, ghost," I said, getting up to clear away my dishes. This one mostly kept to the dining room and it didn't appear very often. It was probably the shade of some long-ago housekeeper or butler making sure I didn't break any rules like feeding cats on the table. The chill disappeared instantly and I was alone again.

I washed my dishes and then wandered around the big house for a while looking for something to do. It was ironic that I was bored when I had this whole fantastic house to myself, but it wasn't the same without people to share it with.

When it was time for the late-night feed, I made sure my crew were tucked away safely in their stalls with a snack and that their water buckets were full, watching hopefully as the other barn workers made small talk with one another and then went back to their staff accommodation one by one, leaving me behind.

Finally, I flicked the lights off and rolled the big barn doors shut. I went wearily back to the house and trudged upstairs to my room, my unfinished novel under one arm and Morris under the other. I deposited them both on the bed and lit a fire in the hearth.

*At least I have my job tomorrow to look forward to*, I reminded myself. The thought was enough to take the edge off the loneliness.

## Chapter 5

*M*orning came much sooner than I'd expected, but I'd laid my clothes out by the fire the day before so all I had to do was leap from bed to hearth and get changed into my pre-warmed breeches and sweater.

"Sorry, Morris," I said, lifting him off my sweater and transporting him back to the bed. He stretched out upside-down with his paws in the air and broke out into a rumbling purr.

I brushed ineffectually at the faint halo of hair he'd left on my clothes then gave up. There was no point in being too particular about it since I was just going to the barn. An unanticipated part of having a housecat was that sometimes they clawed things or shed piles of hair on clothes and furniture, or vomited randomly from time to time. The litter box had taken a bit of getting used to, too. But, even with all that, it was still worth it.

There was no sign of Bally and I guessed that maybe it was too early even for him.

"I'm going to the barn now, Bally," I said into the empty

air, just in case he was listening. "Meet me there if you still want your walk."

The moon was behind a thick bank of clouds and the morning seemed extra-dark somehow without Bally beside me for company. The glow of my headlamp barely cut through the inky blackness.

I was the first one at the barn. I flipped on the lights, silently apologizing to the horses who stood blinking their eyes at the sudden brightness.

"Good morning," I whispered, going up to stroke Lark's nose. "Are you ready for your breakfast?"

Of course she was, they all were, and once I'd fed my five living horses and put hay in Bally's still-empty stall I was faced with a barn full of thirty-five other unfed horses who stared at me hungrily with hopeful expressions. Far down the aisle one of them began to bang a hoof loudly against their stall door and instantly a few of the others followed suit.

*Darn it, I guess I'll have to feed them all.* I couldn't just go about my chores and ignore them while they were hungry. The other grooms wouldn't be out for over an hour yet.

I headed to the feed room and looked at the huge chart on the wall that outlined the meticulous diets that each horse was on. We had four different types of hay in the hay room and everyone got something different. My guys were on a simple diet since they weren't in full work, but some of the hard-working horses were fed the equivalent of five-course meals four times a day.

*Could it be any more complicated?* I muttered, pulling out my phone to take a picture of the chart so I wouldn't have to come back and forth. *No wonder the grooms are always grumbling about being overworked.*

It took a while but finally, I had a barn full of quiet, content horses happily eating their breakfast hay.

Now to clean stalls and get my horses worked. I would be

gone all day and it wouldn't be fair to leave them stuck in their stalls without exercise until I got home. Christoph had agreed to feed my crew lunch, but it would still be a long day for them.

They were a little surprised to be brushed and taken out of their stalls so early in the morning, but nobody put up much of a fuss except Allison.

"Come on, it's just a little exercise and then you can go back to your breakfast," I told her as she stood immobile inside the arena entrance. She laid her ears back and swished her tail angrily, lifting a hind foot in warning.

*Oh, great*, I thought, *hand-walking you should be loads of fun when you're in this mood. I'm liable to lose a limb.*

I stared at her sullen expression and made a decision. I reached up and unclipped my lead line from her halter and then stood back well out of the way.

For a moment she did nothing, and then with a squeal she flung out her hind legs and shot off across the arena, leaping and twisting in the air to celebrate her freedom.

*Don't hurt yourself, don't hurt yourself,* I chanted silently, a little awed by her raw power as she flew around me in wild circles. At first, it looked like she would never stop, but finally, she slowed and then came to an abrupt halt right beside me, her sides heaving.

"Good girl, Allison," I said and she unexpectedly reached out and leaned her sweaty head against my shoulder, pressing into me. I ran my hand down her neck and tugged her ears gently like I used to do with Bally. She didn't object, she just heaved a big sigh and then looked up in the direction of the arena doorway, nickering under her breath.

I followed her glance guiltily, thinking one of the grooms or Christoph had caught me but there was nobody there.

"Come on, let's get you cooled out. Then you can finish the rest of your breakfast in peace."

The grooms began to arrive by the time I finally put Allison away, muttering sleepy hellos as they slouched past me.

"You fed hay already," Sonja said her thick Australian accent. She yawned widely and rubbed her eyes. "Thanks. You're brilliant. Is there coffee yet?"

"No, sorry, I didn't think to put it on."

"First one out makes coffee," she said sharply as she headed to the feed room. "Barn rules."

*The first time I've heard of it*, I thought, and then smiled to myself. *But she did say I was brilliant. That's progress.*

Sonja was one of the riders who'd been lured here with the promise of working with our finely-trained show horses. But instead, she was stuck riding a group of undisciplined young-sters that were liable to buck or spook and dump them on the arena floor without warning.

She was a good rider though, and she instilled confidence into every young horse she rode. I thought maybe she'd be a good match for Allison if she stuck around long enough.

As soon as my horses had been worked and my chores had been done, I rushed back to the house, feeling like I'd already worked a full-time shift before the day had even started.

"Don't bolt your food, Jillian," Betty tut-tutted as I hoovered down my breakfast at record speed, but there was no way I was about to be late for my first day at work.

There was still no sign of Bally and I felt a little worried as I rushed out to my car. What was he up to?

Myrtle cooperated again, two days in a row was beginning to be a habit, and the ghostly presence in the storage shed did little more than rattle a few dusty boxes in the far end of the building as I passed.

The morning sun shone brightly; birds chirped away in the wintery chill no doubt glad that the ever-falling snow had finally stopped.

The drive to town was easy; a plow had miraculously been by in the night and the roads had been scraped and then sprinkled with sand so that I didn't have to careen off the snow-banks to make the turns. I found a parking spot within a block of the bookstore and the slippery sidewalks from yesterday had also been cleared of ice. My day was looking up already.

The sunshine seemed to have put everyone in town in a good mood. People called out hellos as I passed and, startled by all the goodwill, I smiled broadly at everyone I met and called hello back. The hardware store, MapleWood and More, had finally taken down its Christmas display and old Mr. Farner, who ran the place with his wife, was optimistically setting up a spring planting display under his awning.

"Never too early to start thinking about gardening," he said, beaming at me as I passed.

"Absolutely," I agreed, though I'd never gardened in my life. I was just happy he didn't recognize me or at least didn't still hold a grudge against me for being a Harrington. I'd gotten to witness the bitter shouting match between him and Mother when she'd come in person to raise their rent about five years ago. I'd made a point to give the place a wide berth ever since.

"Jillian." Mr. Galinski came to meet me as soon as I stepped inside the bookshop, taking my chilly hands in his. "Right on time, just as I expected. Are you ready to work?"

"Of course," I said, pulling off my coat and scarf and hanging them on the nearby coat rack. "I'm at your service."

First, we had to have a cup of tea together and Mr. Galinski told me excitedly all about the philosophy book he was reading. Then I was set to work dusting and tidying the stacks and putting wayward books back on their shelves.

It took about an hour for Bally to find me and I had never been so relieved to see him. He looked around excitedly, flicking his ears in all directions and gave me a little bump on the arm as if to say he approved of our new arrangements.

He disappeared and then popped up behind the front

counter, bopping his nose against the cash register, making the keys lightly jingle. After that, there was no stopping him from exploring the entire store. He trotted carefully around the bookshelves then dropped his nose to the floor sniffing the bottom of the stacks like a hunting dog looking for rabbits.

"What are you doing?" I whispered, glancing over my shoulder to make sure Mr. Galinski was still occupied in his office. Bally flicked an ear toward me but didn't stop his snuffling.

I went back to stacking the shelves crossing my fingers that he wouldn't knock anything over. After a few minutes, I heard his hooves clopping softly down the hall toward the rare books room.

In the first few hours, there was exactly one customer, a round, apple-cheeked woman looking for an old recipe book, who Mr. Galinski served himself.

"That was Mrs. Whitmore," he said, finding me where I stood perched on the wooden ladder dusting some of the upper shelves. "You'd like her. She makes the most divine cakes."

"Oh." An unpleasant memory hit me and I clutched at the shelf to keep from slipping. "Yes, I remember now, she made my engagement cake."

"Oh, you got married, did you?" Mr. Galinski asked, looking in confusion at my empty ring finger.

"No, but nearly. I dodged *that* bullet. I'm lucky he showed me what a horrible person he was before I married him." The words came out fast before I could think about it.

I looked down at my new boss cautiously, wondering how much he remembered about that day. He must have heard the gossip even if he hadn't been at the party. I was sure *everyone* in town knew how I'd been publicly dumped and abandoned before making it to the altar. I hadn't exactly behaved my best on that day. I'd been a hysterical mess.

"Good riddance to bad rubbish, I say." Mr. Galinski smiled up at me kindly and patted my arm.

I couldn't help but smile back. "Yes, and you're right, the cake *was* delicious."

"She's a good cook and a good woman. We'll have to have her bake something special to celebrate your new job here."

"Oh, I don't think we need to make a big deal—"

"Nonsense, you should rejoice every moment that you're alive on this planet, my girl, every day is a gift."

His expression turned serious but then lightened again in the next moment. "And that means taking every possible opportunity to eat cake."

I thought about what he'd said as I navigated the short distance down the sidewalk to MapleBrew later that afternoon. Maybe I *had* spent too much time focusing on the sad, traumatic parts of my past and not enough time being grateful for the good things in my life. Bally's sacrifice had given me another chance at living; I couldn't go around wasting the moments I had left by shying away from the world and being afraid that I'd get hurt.

Mr. Galinski had told me that every day at two o 'clock he used to send Toby down to MapleBrew to pick up Caramel Macchiatos and cinnamon buns. Now that I was his assistant, it would be my job to collect our treats and bring them back to the shop.

I didn't want to go; it was too soon to see them after my mortifying interview from yesterday, but I couldn't tell him that.

The sun was bright overhead, and the reflection of the snow made me squint and wish I'd worn sunglasses.

The bell jangled over my head and I paused in the open doorway to let my eyes adjust to the dimmer interior. For a second, it looked like seats at the counter were full of customers but when I blinked again, they were empty. Only

Katie stood there, her cheeks flushed and a startled expression on her face.

As I came nearer, she looked down and then swiped her hand rapidly across the counter, knocking something onto the floor at her feet. She didn't stoop to pick it up, though.

"Oh, Jilly," she said in a flustered voice, glancing over her shoulder toward the kitchen for a moment, "come in."

"Mr. Galinski has a cinnamon bun addiction that I'm here to fill," I said, smiling nervously. I glanced around quickly to make sure Kristal wasn't lurking nearby. Maybe that's why Katie was acting so strangely.

"Oh, my gosh, I haven't even gotten your order together yet. It's been so busy here. Can you hang on a second while I get it ready?"

"Of course." The café didn't look busy. Now that the lunch rush was over; it was empty. I picked a seat near the counter, hoping to chat a little more with Katie about horses while she worked. I still had to tell her about my idea.

"So, I spoke with our trainer," I said, feeling a little excited, "and he thought that maybe once you come up and meet the horses there might be a chance for you to ride. One of my mares, Serena, would be a good one to start on …"

"That's nice," Katie said vaguely, not looking up from the whirring coffee machine. The paper cups in her hands trembled slightly as she moved to the counter and set them down. "I like horses."

*Huh?* I raised an eyebrow and took in her flushed cheeks and preoccupied expression.

"Katie, is everything okay?"

"What?" She looked up, startled. "Of course, I'm fine. Everything's good." She finished the drinks, quickly boxed up the cinnamon buns and pushed the box across the counter toward me, waving me away when I reached for my wallet.

"No, don't pay. Mr. G runs a tab here that he pays off every month. I'll just write your order down in the book."

"Thanks, well, um, have a good day." I hesitated, wondering if I should say more about the horses.

"Yep, bye," she said quickly and then disappeared toward the kitchen.

I backed out into the street, balancing my purchases carefully, and tried not to be too disappointed with how the conversation had gone. She was a teenager after all and I'd heard that they could be moody. Still, I'd hoped she'd have been more excited at the thought of riding. She'd seemed so keen when I'd spoken to her about it yesterday. It looked like I might have to come up with another plan to get my crew exercised.

*I should just bite the bullet and ride the easier horses myself,* I thought glumly. *And I'm sure I'd like it again once I got into a routine.* But the idea filled me with dread instead of joy, and I secretly wondered if, in my heart, I'd given up riding for good.

Across the road, there was the sound of screeching tires and I looked up to see a man dodge across the street, narrowly missing being hit by a car.

*Was that Raoul?* I thought in astonishment as the man stumbled into Aspen Ale, the local pub, the door slamming nosily behind him.

I wasn't about to follow him to find out. I would just let Christoph know what I'd seen when I got home.

The bell chimed over my head when I pushed into Curiosity and Mr. Galinski looked up from the counter with a gleam in his eye.

"Ah, the world's best cinnamon buns," he said, coming to meet me and taking the carry-away tray out of my hands. "Thank you, Jillian."

The day passed more quickly after that. Customers drifted in and out of the shop at regular intervals and I was surprised to see how many children and teenagers showed up. They didn't look intimidated by Mr. Galinski as I had been as a kid; in fact, everyone seemed to love him.

"I got an A on my history essay," a thin, dark-haired girl told him, beaming as she pulled a handful of papers out of her battered green backpack. There was a giant A scrawled in red at the top and the words "well done" written next to it. "That was the first A I've ever gotten in my life. I think my mom was in shock."

"I just gave you the idea," he said proudly, "you did all the hard work. You're a smart girl and an excellent writer. I know you'll do great things in life."

Her face lit up even more and she went away humming under her breath.

I was given a lesson on the ancient cash register which would have been much easier if Bally hadn't lodged himself right at my elbow, his warm horsey breath tickling my neck as he stared down with interest at the keys.

Pretty soon I got the hang of it and Mr. G said he was going to his office for a quick nap and left me to handle the front of the shop on my own.

I was feeling ridiculously proud of myself for handling the next few transactions on my own when the front door jangled open and a tall, pale-faced man stepped inside, dragging one of the teenaged boys from yesterday by the arm.

Bally snorted loudly in my ear and gave my arm a little nudge, making me jump.

The man looked at me strangely and then pushed the boy in front of him, keeping one hand gripped tightly on the boy's shoulder.

"Hello," the man said in a smooth voice, smiling at me with his pale lips. "You must be the new assistant. I'm Professor Mason."

"Yes, I'm Jillian," I said hesitantly, struck by the look of abject misery on the boy's face. Professor Mason must be the boy's father; they had the same blonde hair and sharp features, although the man was painfully thin and pale like he'd just come out of a long illness.

*Toby*, I remembered, the boys' name was Toby. I felt a pang of sympathy for him. He'd lost his job and now he was being packed off to military school by an angry father. Still, he *had* been caught stealing, twice. I guessed he'd made his own choices in life.

Bally disappeared and then reappeared beside the boy, sniffing again as he had earlier, his ears swivelling around as if he were trying to solve a confusing puzzle.

The man cleared his throat and I realized that'd he'd been saying something while I was distracted by watching Bally.

"I'm sorry, what did you say?"

"I was asking if you'd had a chance to see the rare books room yet. Sid has a wonderful collection. Lots of local history."

"No, I'm sorry, I haven't yet. It's my first day so I'm just settling in."

"Well, we won't keep you then. I was just stopping in to say goodbye to Sid and to have Toby apologize again. We collected the boy's things this morning, but he wants to make a proper apology for his shocking behaviour."

"Mr. Galinski is still in his office. I think he might be having a nap."

"Well, we won't keep you then. We'll just run back there and have a quick word with him."

The boy sent me an anguished look and then dropped his gaze to the floor as he was dragged away.

I looked after them and repressed a shiver. Sure, the boy had been rude to me yesterday when I'd fallen and he had been caught stealing, but there was something very disquieting about the way this father was treating his son.

"He's almost as bad as Mother, isn't he, Bally?" I asked but the horse was gone.

Since the shop was so quiet, I'd set myself to cleaning and organizing the front counter, putting away the stacked books that didn't need to be there and making a pile of all the miscellaneous paperwork that needed to be filed.

I was so preoccupied with my project that I nearly forgot about Toby and his father until they appeared again nearly an hour later. This time the boy's eyes were red with tears and his face was blotchy. The father looked furious as he dragged his son past me.

"You're a disappointment," he snapped and I jumped thinking for a second he'd meant me. Mother had certainly said similar things to me on many occasions.

"Dad, I'm sorry … I just can't be who you want me to be."

Their words were cut off as the father dragged his son outside.

*What on earth was that about?* I thought uneasily. They'd left so angrily … especially when Professor Mason had said that they were just there to apologize. Something didn't seem right.

I put down the cloth I was using to polish the counter and walked back through the shop to the office.

"Mr. Galinski?" I asked hesitantly, pushing open the half-closed door. But the room was empty.

I turned around slowly, wondering what to do next as the uneasy feeling in the pit of my stomach grew and grew until I was a bundle of jangling nerves.

A faint smell of burning filled the air and the hair on the back of my neck prickled. There was a light, cold touch on my hand and something gave my fingers a little tug.

*A ghost*, I thought, repressing a shiver. *It's trying to get my attention.*

The tug came again, this time harder and I stepped forward, letting it pull me across the room toward a large grey filing cabinet. As soon as I reached it, the smell of burning intensified and then disappeared completely. The cold feeling was gone too.

*What did you want me to find?* I thought, reaching out to touch the cabinet gently. It shivered under my touch and then moved a few inches, swinging outward toward me.

I stepped back in astonishment. It wasn't a cabinet at all; it was a door in disguise. There was a whole other room hidden behind it.

It swung open fully and I was shocked to see that inside was a make-shift laboratory of sorts. The small room had counters on all sides and two long tables in the middle. Lots of complicated equipment sat on one of the tables. Cords ran everywhere and one machine made a clicking, whirring noise as a wheel spun slowly on the top. Glass vessels filled with various coloured liquids sat bubbling on the other table. Long tubes connected some of them and one tube filled with blue liquid ran back to the whirring machine and disappeared somewhere inside.

*What in the world is all this?* I thought in astonishment.

"Oh dear," said an anxious, wavery voice behind me and I spun around to see my boss standing in the office doorway, a large, leather-bound book clutched to his chest. "You shouldn't be in here."

"I'm sorry," I said quickly, backing a few steps away from him. "I was just trying to find you. I didn't mean to open it. Honestly. I touched the cabinet by accident and it swung open."

That wasn't quite the truth, but it was as close as I could get without telling him about the ghostly presence.

He stared at me with large, worried eyes and shook his head.

"I've made a grave mistake, Jillian," he said. "I'm a foolish, sentimental old man."

I gulped, watching his wild expression with alarm. He

looked much different than the kind, elderly man who'd hired me. A shiver of fear ran down my spine.

"This is all happening so fast," he muttered. "I need more time. I've come this far and I'm so close to the end."

His breath came out in short gasps and any worry I'd had for my safety disappeared.

"So close to what?" I said gently, stepping toward him and laying a hand on his arm to comfort him. "What's the matter?"

"My discovery, the meaning of life, the …"

He broke off and looked down at the ground. "I suppose I was never meant to make the final discovery," he said sadly. "My life's work was always meant to be passed on, just as it was by my mother before me."

"Why don't I make you some tea," I said soothingly, and I was relieved when he nodded and followed me obediently into the hall, still clutching the book. I sat him down in the little alcove and then went to plug in the kettle.

"Do you believe in fate, Jillian?" he asked, once I'd brought him a steaming cup of tea. He carefully set the book down on the table and laid his hand gently against the cover. A strange symbol was embossed on the front, a circle inside a square inside a triangle inside a larger circle.

"I … I don't know. I've never thought about it."

"It was impeccable timing that you ended up at my door looking for a job just when I needed an assistant. Just when I needed the *right* assistant."

"Um, I suppose …"

"Just when I'm in the final stretch of completing my life's work, I happened to come across a relative of the very man who set me on this path. You."

"Oh?" I said warily, the hairs on the back of my neck beginning to prickle. I repressed a shiver and glanced toward to front door, making sure we were still alone.

"Greystone was built before the town of Maplegrove existed you know," he said suddenly.

"Yes," I said cautiously, "it was."

My ancestors had started coming here before Canada was even a country by modern standards. Mother always said that they'd built Greystone as a sanctuary from the outside world when they'd had to flee suddenly from Europe.

"Your ancestors were quite the widely travelled bunch, and highly connected, too. Prince Arthur and his entourage were almost regular guests in the late 1800s and early 1900s."

"Oh, right," I said vaguely. "I think there's a painting of him in the dining room and there are some old sepia photos somewhere in the library. He visited with his wife, right? Or was it his mistress?"

"It depended on the time of year," Mr. Galinski said seriously. "But it's not *who* he brought with him that's important; rather it was *what* he brought with him."

"What do you mean?"

"At that time, Greystone was a bit of a well-defended fortress."

"Really? We barely remember to lock the front door nowadays."

"It's best not to advertise that fact," he said sharply, "and for pity's sake, lock it up. All the doors, and the windows too. Especially in these uncertain times. Most people are good, Jillian, but those who aren't good tend to be very, very bad."

His eyes had that wild look again and he rubbed a hand feverishly across his forehead.

"Anyway, as I was saying, a good many influential people from all over the world trekked to Greystone at all times of the year. It would have been a rough, uncomfortable journey in those days, but for some reason, they continued to make the trip. It was said that many of them arrived with treasures from far parts of the globe."

"Oh, yes, we have quite a few things on display."

"Some things are meant to be on display and some things are meant to be hidden."

He stared at me hard as if I were supposed to guess his cryptic meaning.

"Well, we keep the valuable stuff locked up in the …"

"No," he said sharply, "don't tell me. I don't need to know."

"Um, okay," I said, taken a little aback by his abrupt manner. It wasn't like I expected him to break in and steal some ancient, dusty artifacts. Anything of real value was kept in vaults at the bank or locked away in the home safe. Not even I had the key to that.

"I can't keep telling this story properly if you interrupt me, Jillian." He raised his eyebrows at me and then took a sip of tea before continuing. "As more and more settlers moved to the area, the town slowly grew up around Greystone.

Gossip travelled about the frequency of important visitors to the manor. Rumours started that many of these visitors arrived with valuable treasures and departed with either money or different treasures. And that maybe these items might not have been purchased by completely legal channels."

"Smugglers," I said in surprise. It was the first I'd heard of it, but I wouldn't put anything past my family.

"Exactly. Traders in valuable goods, let's just say. And Greystone may have also been a place to hide important items and documents that might be of interest to darker characters."

"Like what, exactly?"

Mr. Galinski shrugged. "Political documents, maps, family trees, anything that needed to be temporarily hidden but was too important to be outright destroyed."

He fell silent, staring moodily down at the teacup between his hands.

"One of my ancestors on my mother's side arrived here not

that many years after Greystone was built. He was a young scholar named Simon who had apprenticed with a local Apothecary and then went on to marry a local girl. He was hard working and honest in his trade, but his real love was books."

He paused and stared off in the distance while I waited impatiently for him to go on.

"One night, when he was closing up shop a stranger stumbled in the door clutching a leather-bound book to his chest. He'd been running from someone; his clothes were torn, he was filthy and exhausted and had a deep wound in his side. He wouldn't say who he was but he begged Simon for help and shelter.

"Simon had made an oath to help others when he became an Apothecary and he took his duties seriously. Despite the man's desperate experience, Simon decided to help him. He bandaged his wounds, gave him food and drink, and let the man rest. He planned to ask the stranger his business in the morning and, if it turned out that the man was a criminal then he'd turn him over to the authorities.

"Only Simon never got the chance. When he woke in the morning the man was gone but at the end of his bed, he'd left behind the book and a note.

"*Guard this book with your very soul,* the note read, *for in it you will find the key to everlasting life.*

"Simon hid the book in a secret room in his shop, fully intending to turn it over to the authorities once he'd had a chance to read it and discuss things over with his wife, who always had good advice.

"But his plans were cut short when the stranger's body was found floating in the river, a dagger buried in his throat.

"He waited anxiously for someone to come looking for the book, but when the knock on the door never came, he began to read it in secret. He discovered that it was a textbook of sorts, part scientific manual and part philosophical treatise. And the words revealed a fantastic new world for him, a mixture of science and magic blended seamlessly; the mystery of Alchemy."

*Alchemy?* I thought, my skin prickling suddenly. *Isn't that the search for immortality? Is that what Mr. Galinski is working on in his creepy secret room?*

"Studying the book and devoting himself to the work became his greatest joy. In time, when he took his son on as an apprentice, he initiated the boy into the Alchemist's way as well. And that boy, when he grew up, initiated his son and so on. The Apothecary shop turned into a bookstore, and that building is the one you're in now. The lineage passed down until it was time for my mother Fiona to be initiated, and in turn, she taught the way to me."

"Okay," I said slowly, "it's a great story, but what does this have to do with my family?"

"When my ancestor Simon lived, there were two Harrington heirs."

"Oh right, they were twins and one died of influenza …" I broke off as the older man sent me a stern look.

"Please refrain from interrupting again," he said. "We're coming to the important part. As I said there were *two heirs*. Twins. They were very close and shared the same curiosity about the natural world as well as a love for exploration and travel. As young teenagers, they took many voyages abroad and one particular trip changed their lives."

I leaned forward but said nothing. I knew enough about my family history to guess that this story was probably going to end badly, at least for my ancestors.

"It was in a small village in deepest India that they first met the alchemist. They were on an archeological dig and had wandered away from the group. The second they met the man they knew that their perception of the world had been forever changed."

Mr. Galinski paused and lifted his teacup to his lips with trembling fingers. I noticed for the first time how pale he looked, like all the colour had been drained out of him.

"Mr.G, are you sure you're all right …"

"The thing about *true* students of alchemy," My boss went on as if I hadn't spoken, "is that they might start out searching for treasure, adventure, and everlasting life, but somewhere during their studies, they realize that they themselves are the ones being transformed. That is the true gift of alchemy. Gaining wisdom, compassion and the ability to connect with the divine universe."

He was quiet for a moment, lost in thought. "It is said that the secrets will only be revealed to one who is not working for their own gain. It is only through helping others, through a quest for a greater good, that the magic is unlocked.

"August Harrington had always been much quieter and introspective than his twin Gregory. It was not long before his studies in alchemy led him more to the spiritual path, while Gregory's sole aim was to find the secret of turning lead into gold and especially in creating an elixir for everlasting life.

"They had both studied together in India with the Alchemist for two years and when the man died suddenly in a monsoon, they brought all his books and equipment back with them to Greystone.

"Gregory was by nature more outgoing and was often seen riding his horses through the village or out hunting in the woods. August, in contrast, became very much a hermit and spent most of his time locked in his study reading and conducting experiments. The villagers nearly forgot he existed at all.

"Gregory grew impatient with the slow progress of the work and set out on a journey around the world to visit other alchemists to see if there was a way to speed up the process. He enjoyed a lavish lifestyle and wanted to make sure he could enjoy it in the manner he was accustomed to for many years to come. Forever, if he had his way. Meanwhile, August stayed home to study in peace.

"One year later, August stumbled into my ancestor Simon's Apothecary begging for help. The next day he was found in the river with a dagger buried in his chest."

"No," I said in surprise, "that isn't how the story ended. Gregory came back from travelling just in time to say goodbye to August, who was already on his deathbed from influenza."

"Maybe in *your* family history books," Mr. Galinski said dryly, "but not in the ones I've read. Many people witnessed August being dragged from the river. And he hadn't died from any influenza.

"It didn't take long for Simon to realize who his murdered stranger was and he knew better than to mention the book to anyone. Gradually, he pieced the story together and it was his theory that August had been murdered by his twin."

"Murdered?" I exclaimed. "But why?"

"Simon believed that Gregory had come back from his travels with a very particular item that would speed up the process of creating the elixir of life by decades. It was a dark process though, a perversion of the holy path usually travelled by an alchemist, and something a true master would never attempt. August must have known that what Gregory proposed was evil and had tried to escape his twin, taking the book with him. Without the book, Gregory would never be able to create the elixir on his own, he hadn't studied the art with nearly as much dedication as August; he needed it badly."

Mr. Galinski fell silent and I too stayed quiet, mulling over his strange story.

"Oh dear," he said suddenly, "look at the time. I need to get to an appointment with my lawyer, I'm afraid. Things have changed most abruptly. I hate to leave you with the shop on your first day, but I won't be long and you'll be all right, won't you?"

"Oh, yes of course," I said startled, still thinking about alchemy, "but wait, what was the object that Gregory brought back to Greystone?"

"Object?" he said, rising hastily to his feet and heading to the front of the shop for his hat and coat.

"Yes." I stood up and trailed after him. "You said he had something with him that sped up the elixir of life thing. Something that August didn't like."

"Oh, yes, it was some trifle or another. A carved statue I believe."

"But …"

The bell jangled as he yanked the door open and stepped out into the snow. "Take care of the shop like it was your own," he called and shut the door firmly behind him.

*Well, now that was bizarre,* I thought, glad that I was alone at last with my thoughts. I wished Nanny was here so I could talk it over with her. She knew a lot about my family history and could verify which version of August's death was the truth. I couldn't wait to get home and ask her about it. There were a few old local books at home that had been written around the same time; I could go over them tonight and see if I could find any clues.

*And why had the ghost dragged me to the secret door in the first place?* I wondered. *Why did it want me to see the laboratory so badly?*

## Chapter 6

*S*trange to say but the day was pretty normal after that. I washed our tea things in the little sink and stacked everything neatly away then went back to my project of organizing the front counter.

A few more customers came in and I managed to successfully find their books, take their money, and give back mostly the correct change.

Mr. Galinski came back a few hours later, looking much happier than when he'd left and gave me a friendly smile as he stepped inside.

"You've done good work today, Jillian," he said kindly. "I hope that discovering my little hobby hasn't put you off of working here. You're an asset to the store."

"Of course not," I said, returning his smile. "I love it here."

"Excellent, well, time for you to head home then. It will be dark soon. Goodnight."

I hummed happily under my breath as I made my way out to Myrtle in the growing dusk. The sky was already a deep shade of inky purple and the streetlights had come on.

Myrtle was parked a few doors down from the shop, in the

shadows, and I instinctively slowed as I approached her, my skin prickling with the sense that there was someone, or maybe some*thing*, lurking there. Was it a human or a ghost?

"Hello, Jilly," Katie called, stepping away from my car. She was dressed in breeches and tall boots and wearing a thick, warm coat. She had an oversized brown bag slung over her shoulder that I guessed contained her riding helmet and clothes to change into. "I had to run home and get my stuff, but I'm all ready now."

"Ready for what?" I said in bewilderment. "I didn't realize you wanted to come *tonight*. You didn't seem that interested when I talked about riding today."

"Oh yeah, sorry about that," she said quickly. "I was distracted by, uh, some stuff. I want to meet the horses. Can I come over tonight? Please?"

All I wanted to do was go home and relax and think about the story Mr. Galinski had told me, but I looked at her eager face and relented with a sigh. After all, the horses still had to be worked tonight one way or another. I might as well give Katie a try now rather than later so I could let Christoph know if he needed to start looking for yet another working student to hire.

"Sure. I guess it's okay. But I'll have to feed dinner and do chores first before we do any riding. They'll be hungry."

"That's okay. I'll help you with everything, I don't mind. Thank you so much for letting me visit Greystone. I've been looking forward to this for a long time."

She was all smiles when she hopped into Myrtle's passenger seat. If she hadn't seemed enthusiastic earlier today, she was more than making up for it now. She chattered excitedly non-stop all the way back to Greystone, hardly taking a breath the whole way. She told me about the stable where she'd worked before and gave me a detailed report of every single horse and pony she'd ridden in the last twelve years. I hadn't spent that much time around teenagers before but it was exhausting.

Thankfully the drive to Greystone wasn't long. I parked Myrtle right out front of the barn, realizing belatedly that I would have to drive Katie home again afterward and wondering how exactly I'd gotten roped into this visit.

My irritation faded though as soon as we stepped through the barn doors. Katie's expression lit up when she saw the horses and her nervous chatter came to an abrupt halt.

"Oh," she said breathlessly, "it's so beautiful."

I had to agree with her. Even though it was old, the stable at Greystone was magnificent. The aisle was huge, big enough to drive one of the hay rigs right through, and paved with interlocking white bricks that drew the eye down to the end of the expanse. Between the broodmares, the horses in training, the young stock, and one ghost horse, we had over forty animals housed here.

The outside of the stable was made of stone, but the inside was fashioned from honey-coloured polished wood. Black metal bars covered the top half of the oversized stalls that lined the aisle on either side, with openings over each stall door so the horses could stick their heads out. The left half of the aisle was given completely over to the horses living quarters. On the right was a spacious tack room, a feed room, a huge bay for storing hay and, of course, the indoor arena. We didn't have a loft upstairs like some barns. Instead, we had an open cathedral ceiling that stretched way up so you could see the old wood and stone archway that had stood there for almost two hundred years.

For a barn, it was spotless; the aisles were always swept clean of hay and dirt, the stalls were kept immaculate and full of knee-high shavings, and it was someone's job to rub down all the exposed wood with lemon oil twice a week.

Katie inhaled appreciatively, taking in the mixed scents of horse and leather, hay and lemon. A smile lit her face.

The barn was laid out with the show horses and top sale

horses at the front of the barn nearest the door, then the horses in training, the young stock, and then the broodmares had the extra-large stalls at the furthest end of the barn.

Before my injury last fall, I'd been a showing-machine, winning ribbons by the bucketful with my crew of five. So that meant my horses had the top spot by the door with Gil's horses beside mine, then Christoph's younger horses.

If Mother hadn't left in a huff after I'd come out of the hospital, my unused horses would have been demoted to the farthest depths of the stable within a month. But, without her here, nobody cared; it was too much of a hassle to keep moving horses around. So, fat and out of shape as they were, my guys were still the first horses Katie approached.

"Oh, Jilly, are these all yours?" she asked, looking in wonder down the aisle. She went slowly, almost reverently, up to Serena and held out her hand for the mare to sniff. Serena was a matronly sort of horse and not shy. She lipped at Katie's hand to see if there might be a treat and then reached out and blew her breath in Katie's hair.

"She likes me," Katie said incredulously.

"Of course she does. Why wouldn't she? Come on, let's feed first."

Having an extra set of hands was nice. Katie helped me carry hay to everyone and then we mixed up the evening grain for us to feed after each horse had been exercised. Once the animals were busy eating, we brought out a wheelbarrow and cleaned the stalls one by one.

Katie was a different person than the one she'd been earlier today. The horses had cast a spell of serenity over her and she hummed happily under her breath as she worked. She also didn't say a word when I put hay into Bally's empty stall and topped up his water bucket, though I caught her sending me a side-long glance when she thought I wasn't looking.

Bally wasn't back yet and I wondered if he was still sniffing around the bookstore. He sure had seemed to enjoy it there.

We moved into Serena's stall and let the mare munch her hay while we brushed her and put her tack on. Katie hadn't been lying about having been around horses in the past. She was quiet and efficient and knew how to correctly put Serena's gear on without asking questions.

She only faltered once we were leading the mare to the arena.

"Are you sure that it's okay for me to ride her?" she asked, twisting the reins between her fingers anxiously. "She's probably better trained than the horses I used to ride, and it's been over a year since I sat on a horse, I don't want to ruin her."

"You'll be fine," I assured her, "Serena is easy-going; I think she'd be perfect for you."

Katie's anxious look melted a little once she was mounted on Serena's broad back. After a few laps around the ring, she let out a sigh and her entire body relaxed. Serena felt the change in her rider and instead of shambling along half-asleep, she arched her neck and strode forward with purpose.

"Oh, she's lovely," Katie said, her face lighting up into a smile.

I let them walk around and get used to each other, having them do all sizes of circles and loops to get them both loosened up.

"Do you remember how to ask for a leg yield?" I asked and when Katie nodded, I had them practice moving sideways gently across the ring. Serena quietly mouthed the bit as she bent her body slightly around Katie's leg.

*Her hands are light on the reins and she's a naturally balanced rider*, I thought as they moved into a nice, forward trot, *the rest just needs to be polished up. I think she'll be a great fit around here eventually.*

Katie was all smiles after the ride, petting Serena's neck over and over and kissing the mare's silky grey nose.

"Thank you so much for letting me ride," she said as we gave the mare a good grooming and put her blanket on. "That was amazing."

"Do you have time for one more?" I asked, thinking of how well she and Lilo would get along.

"Really? I mean, yes, absolutely. Thank you."

She glanced down at her watch and then froze, her face going pale.

"Oh my gosh, I had no idea what time it was. I was supposed to meet someone. I'm sorry, Jilly, I'll have to go."

She looked at me wide-eyed, her whole body trembling.

"Okay," I said, a little taken aback by her change in manner. "Let me just put Serena away and I can drive you …"

"No, no, that's all right," she said, pushing Serena's lead rope into my hand and backing away. "He was going to pick me up here. I said I'd meet him at the end of the driveway."

"Katie, you can't walk all that way …"

But she turned and trotted out into the night without a backward glance, only pausing to scoop up her duffle bag from the place where she'd left it near the door.

I was about to follow her but just then a truck and trailer crunched up the driveway and I forgot everything else.

*No, it can't be,* I thought, elation surging through me as I recognized our huge six-horse trailer. Gil was back weeks early. From somewhere inside a deep neigh rang out as our stallion Coconut realized that he was home.

The driver's side door opened and Gil jumped out, his face lighting up as he caught sight of me.

"You're back!" I cried, not bothering to hide how happy I was. All I wanted to do was wrap my arms around him and never let go.

We took a few steps toward each other before stopping awkwardly just short of touching. We stared at each other, grinning like idiots.

"It's … um, good to see you," Gil said, clearing his throat. "You look … good."

"You do too," I said and we kept staring until Serena impatiently stomped her foot and began dragging me toward her stall where the rest of her dinner was waiting.

"Wait," Gil laughed, then reached out to snag the mare's reins before grabbing me into a tight hug. I was crushed up against him for two heartbeats and for just that second every single thing was right with the world. Then we broke apart, breathless and smiling. There were so many things I wanted to say.

Coconut called again from the trailer and a chorus of neighs from the barn answered him back.

"I'd better go get him," Gil said. "The big baby has been missing home."

"Is that why you're back early?"

"Partly. I missed home too. And Heinrich had to go to Germany unexpectedly so I thought I might as well come back.

I put Serena away, fumbling a little in my haste to get back to Gil's side. Serena flicked an ear toward me in irritation and I took a breath, forcing myself to slow down and focus on her properly rather than rushing.

"Who was that I saw leaving?" Gil asked as he made sure Coconut's stall was ready and then headed back toward the trailer. "She seemed in a hurry."

"Just a girl from town that I was thinking of getting to ride for us sometimes. Her name is Katie. She did a good job riding Serena, but she's a little strange. I'm not sure if it will work out."

"Hmm, well, it would be nice if it does. We sure need extra help around here."

He waited until I'd untacked the mare and then we walked together out into the snow to unload the trailer. Despite his neighing earlier, Coconut stepped off casually as if he'd been gone a few hours rather than over a month and stopped to sniff my hands and pockets, looking for treats.

"Hello, handsome," I said, "I missed you. I missed both of you. It just wasn't the same here while you were gone."

Gil looked up and sent me a warm smile before turning and leading the big horse into the barn.

"Hey," I said, trotting behind to keep up with them. "Do you want to come over for dinner tonight? I have to tell you all about my new job and I want to hear about your trip. How did Coconut do?"

I stopped short of saying how lonely I was in that big house, even with Bally and Nanny to keep me company and how every day without him had been painful. I could at least *pretend* not to be needy and desperate for someone to talk to.

His face lit up and then fell again. "Sorry, I can't. I already said I'd have dinner with my dad tonight. We have some things to discuss that can't wait. But next time I will. Coconut was fantastic by the way. Heinrich says he's capable of a lot more than what we've been asking of him."

"That's great," I said brightly, doing my best to mask my disappointment that he wasn't coming over. Not needy, not desperate at all. Totally a mature adult capable of handling rejection over here.

"How is it going with the notebooks?" Gil said unexpectedly. "Did you find them yet?"

"Not yet. I've looked in a few places and I've made some lists. It might have to wait until the snow melts before I can search properly."

Gil nodded but didn't say anything more about it.

I helped him unload all his gear from the trailer and put it away and then reluctantly went back to working with the rest of my horses, wishing that Katie had stuck around long enough to help me with a few more.

I did my best to concentrate while I finished brushing

Serena and put her blankets on but it was hard not to have a tiny bit of my attention tuned in to where Gil was working in the barn. It felt like he was a magnet drawing my gaze back to him over and over. All I wanted to do was reassure myself that he was home and not going away again.

I was completely aware of how ridiculous I was feeling but there wasn't much I could do about it

"Have a good night then," Gil called out from the edge of the arena as I heading to the arena to lunge Lilo. "See you tomorrow."

"Okay, bye," I called back, my heart sinking. Tomorrow seemed like a long way away.

I finished working everyone and then made sure they were all settled for the night. I was just about to leave the barn when I heard footsteps behind me.

"Gil?" I turned around happily, thinking he'd changed his mind but instead Raoul stood there, his face pale. I glanced down at the bottle in his hand and frowned.

"Hello," I said cautiously, "what are you doing out here?"

He didn't answer at first, just kept his gaze on me while he took a long swig from his bottle. "Checking on the horses. It's part of this crappy job."

"Raoul," I said quietly, "if you don't like your job then you should give notice. You don't seem happy here."

"Yeah, you'd like it if I quit, wouldn't you?"

*Yes,* I thought, keeping a neutral expression on my face. *Very much.*

"I wouldn't like being short-staffed, again," I said as calmly as I could, "but I don't think you should stay here if you don't like it."

"Well, what else would I do with my life? All I know is horses."

"I know how you feel," I said, softening toward him a little, "believe me. But there are so many other things …"

"Don't give me advice, rich girl. You don't know anything about my life. I see the way you look down on me, princess. You all do. Everyone in this town. Even that stupid girl in the coffee shop thinks she's something for kicking me out of that dump, just because I was a little tipsy."

I frowned. Had Katie or Kristal had to kick Raoul out of MapleBrew?

"Raoul, nobody looks down on you. But if you're going to drink in the middle of the day—"

"I have to," he said forcefully. "I couldn't stand it here otherwise. But I won't be here forever. I have plans. I made a very good deal tonight, in fact. I traded one old piece of paper for one thousand other pieces of paper. What do you think of that?"

"Um, I have no idea what you're talking about."

"No, you don't, Jilly. Because you're not as clever as you think you are. I know people who can make things happen for me now. Powerful people."

"All right, well, that's nice, Raoul. But I think you're not yourself right now and you should go sleep it off. You can't be drunk around the horses. Christoph won't allow it and neither will I..."

"Whatever. Fine, you do night check then. I'm going to bed."

My hands shook a little as I watched him walk back toward the staff house. I hated to admit it but he'd spooked me. I didn't like feeling scared for my safety, or the horses' safety, on my own property. When I was sure he was gone I fled back to the house as fast as I could.

*He's just a harmless idiot*, I tried to reassure myself, *but we can't let him stay if he's going to act like this. I'll have to talk to Christoph.*

I hated to lose another rider and stable hand but Raoul was clearly spiralling downward fast.

## Chapter 7

*I* paused just outside the kitchen entrance to scrape the snow off my boots and frowned, noticing that a sliver of light from the open door was shining onto the mat outside.

*That's strange, Betty's left the door open. That's completely unlike her.*

I stepped inside and shut the door behind me only to have it bounce open again. What the heck? Something was jammed just inside the sill, keeping it from closing.

I knelt and saw that a small chunk of frozen snow was lodged in the doorjamb.

*It's out of someone's boot,* I thought, frowning as I dug the piece out with my fingers. The small chunk was flattened on one side and had a zig-zagged pattern embossed into the frozen edge. I tossed it outside, a feeling of uneasiness stirring in my stomach.

It was a silly thing really, but it wasn't *my* boot print and I was pretty sure it wasn't Betty's, either. None of the other staff would be here this late.

*Don't be ridiculous,* I told myself firmly, *she's had a service worker in to fix something or maybe it was a delivery driver. You're just spooked because you're alone in this house.*

Resolutely, I shut the door behind me and locked it, then peeled off my layers of winter-wear.

The kitchen smelled delicious and, despite me insisting that I could feed myself, Betty had left dinner and a huge slice of pie warming in the oven, and there was a note on the table congratulating me on my first day of work, and reminding me that she had bridge club again and that she wouldn't be back until after ten o 'clock.

I pulled my dinner out of the oven and set it on the table, rubbing my hands together with glee. Beef Wellington, mashed potatoes slathered in butter and gravy and a side of vegetables; despite my newfound independence, there was no way I was turning down a meal like this.

There was a loud thump in the hall just as I took my first bite and I stiffened, holding my breath and listening intently.

"Mew, mew, meow?" Morris trotted into the room and jumped up into the chair beside me, rubbing his chin excitedly on the edge of the table as he stared fixedly at my dinner.

"Morris, you scared me. And you're begging. Your table manners are awful."

"Mew," he said unapologetically and reached out a big, hairy paw to tap the edge of my plate.

I cut off a tiny piece of meat and set it on the table in front of him, glad Betty wasn't there to witness this.

He ate his meat quickly, licked his chops and sat down to wash his orange ruff with a contented air while I finished the rest of my dinner undisturbed.

"There's even pie, Morris," I told him, pulling the blueberry pie out of the oven and closing my eyes in bliss as I bit into it. "Gil doesn't know what he's missing."

Morris looked up at me and blinked a few times. Then he

turned his head sharply as if he were listening to something deep within the house and got up and trotted into the hall.

*It's just the ghosts*, I told myself, *Bally's probably back upstairs.* I put my dishes into the dishwasher and headed up to my room through the half-darkened hallway, eager for a hot bath and to change into something more comfortable.

Just as I reached the foot of the stairs, there was a cold, tingling feeling against my skin and I paused with one hand on the railing, my glance caught by a small flash of white a few steps up, tucked against the banister. I leaned down and picked up the innocuous chunk of snow and froze, all my senses suddenly on high alert.

*Someone is in the house*, I thought, my heart thundering in my chest. *I need to get out of here.*

But I couldn't move. The back of my neck prickled and I stayed rooted in place. Gradually the panic subsided and I took a deep breath and was able to think properly again.

I looked down at Morris who was sitting at the foot of the stairs beside me, staring up at me with a bemused expression. Wouldn't he be acting more upset if there was a stranger in the house somewhere?

*You're being silly*, I told myself. *It's just a chunk of snow and there is probably a perfectly logical explanation. There isn't anyone here but you and Morris. Now, go get your phone from where you left it in your jacket pocket and then you can decide logically what to do next.*

"Right, Morris," I said out loud, "there is no need to panic."

I held my breath walking back to the kitchen, half-expecting someone to leap out at me from the shadowy hallway. Even the kitchen was full of cupboards and pantries where a thief could hide. Nothing happened of course, and I rescued my phone and headed upstairs.

Part of me wanted nothing more than to call Gil and ask him to come over. But I resisted the temptation. I didn't want to be *that* girl who needed him to save me from my own imagination. He'd just come home and was tired after his long journey. He didn't need to be bothered by me being scared of the dark.

I marched down the hall to my room, flicking on the lights at both the top and the bottom of the stairs so that the entire hallway on both floors was lit up.

Morris had beat me upstairs and was already curled up in the middle of my bed having a wash and I sat down beside him.

"Nanny? Bally?" I asked into the empty air. After a moment Nanny's chair began to rock back and forth quietly, not in an agitated way.

I exhaled in relief. If Nanny was calmly rocking then there wasn't anything dangerous in the house; I was sure of it. Just my imagination acting up again.

*I really should look into getting a dog*, I thought, crawling into bed, *a big one with big teeth. Wouldn't Mother be thrilled to come home and find that waiting for her?*

It had been a long, exciting day, and despite my earlier anxiety, I was able to fall to sleep without any trouble at all.

## Chapter 8

$\mathscr{I}$ was woken in the middle of the night by the covers being rudely yanked off my bed.

"Gak," I said, sitting up abruptly. "Bally, what on earth are you doing? That isn't funny."

He didn't look like he was playing a prank this time though. He tossed his head up and down and neighed anxiously, then pawed hard at the floor.

"Stop," I cried as a piece of hardwood splintered under the force of his hoof and flew off into the corner. This was something new; he'd never destroyed things before. He'd been able to lift small objects on occasion but never do damage.

He looked down at his hoof and snorted, as if he were just as surprised as I was and then turned to the door, looking anxiously at me over his shoulder.

"You want me to follow you? Where are we going?"

He stomped a foot again and I hurried out of bed, automatically throwing on a sweater and breeches. I glanced at the clock; it was three in the morning.

I barely had time to throw on my winter boots and jacket

before the front door banged open of its own accord and Bally hustled me out into the snow.

I hadn't thought to grab a flashlight but Bally's silver coat glowed so brightly that I didn't need it. I automatically headed toward the barn, thinking that the emergency must be there, but Bally cut in front of me, gave me a sharp nudge on the hip and stared hard in the opposite direction.

I stopped and looked at him, wondering what on earth he wanted from me. He stared right back, probably wondering why I was being so dense and then turned and trotted up the hill toward our usual spot.

*Oh, my gosh, if he just woke me up to go on a walk, I'm going to kill him. Again.*

He trotted quickly ahead until we got to the top of a little knoll where a clump of trees grew tight together, all leaning sideways because of the winds that blew across this hilltop all winter long; he stopped and snorted hard.

"What is it, boy?" I said cautiously, following the direction of his pricked ears. The space between the trees was so dark I just barely made out the small, still shape that lay in the hollow area inside. At Bally's nudging, I crept forward.

There was a faint moan and I froze then darted ahead and knelt beside the still body.

"Mr. Galinski?" I said in astonishment, reaching out to touch his side, but before I could he rolled onto his back and between his trembling, bloodied fingers I could just make out the shadowy hilt of a knife buried in his chest.

"Jillian ..." he wheezed, "protect the book, find the page ... destroy the blade ..."

He stopped and gave a mighty gasp. I reached out but just as my fingers touched his coat it dissolved into nothing and then the rest of him disappeared too, his face last of all.

"... protect the book," his lingering voice said and then there was silence.

"Oh, quick, Bally," I said tearfully, "Mr. Galinski. He needs help."

I scrambled to my feet, turning to run back down the hill. My only thought was to somehow start Myrtle and drive into town, but I only made it a few feet before there was a flash of light in front of me and a flurry of whirling snow.

I didn't even have time to think about what happened next. One second, I was knee-deep in snow and the next I was somehow on Bally's broad, and oh so familiar, back and we were flying across the fields, faster than we ever had when he was alive. The still-sleeping town came upon us before I could hardly blink, and then there I was, standing outside Curiosity's front door by myself, dressed in my breeches and without a key, cellphone or a plan.

"Bally?" I hissed, looking around for him but I was all alone, shivering in the snow under the bookstore awning.

"Heeeelp," came the faintest voice from inside.

Only then did I notice that the small pane of glass nearest the door handle had been shattered. What was left of the door swung open at my touch and I crept uneasily into the dark shop and fumbled along the side wall for the light switch. But when my fingers finally found it, nothing happened. The power was out.

I paused, waiting for my eyes to adjust to the moonlight that filtered in through the big windows. The sight that met my eyes would be emblazoned in my mind for the rest of my life.

Poor Mr. Galinski lay with his eyes half open and his breathing coming in shallow gasps. His hands lay on his chest, his fingers lightly clutching something between them and as I drew closer, I sucked my breath in, tears welling in my eyes.

Between his hands was the hilt of a blade that had been buried in his chest. He'd been stabbed but the worst part was that even in the low light, I recognized the weapon very, very well.

*The Serpent's Blade*, I thought in shock and disbelief. The moonlight glinted off the intricately carved hilt, and I imagined that I could see the snake's red eyes staring maliciously at me in the darkness. I had no idea how or why it could have gotten here. Last I'd checked, it had been safely locked in its display case.

I wiped away the tears stinging my eyes and knelt beside my boss, reaching out gingerly to check for a pulse. His skin was cool and dry and felt papery thin, and as I touched him his eyes flickered open and he sent me a gentle smile.

"Jillian," he said softly, wheezing a little, "I ... knew you'd come. Take the key. Find the ..."

"Just hang on, Mr. Galinski," I whispered tearfully, "I'm going to call the ambulance for you. You're going to be okay."

He blinked and reached out a bloodstained finger to gently brush the back of my hand. "The key ... is everything. Get the key."

"Sure, I will, but right now you need help—"

I broke off as he suddenly gripped my wrist with a startlingly strong grasp and gave my hand a yank. I looked down and saw that he'd managed to draw a gold chain out of his pocket and he now pressed it tightly into my hand.

"Run," he said. And then his eyes closed and his hand fell lifelessly to the floor.

*No!* I stared at him in helpless astonishment, hoping against hope that he'd just passed out and wasn't dead.

"Please don't die," I told him, stuffing the key hastily into my pocket. I jumped up and ran to the phone next to the cash register. But when I lifted the receiver there wasn't a dial tone. Right, it was one of those cordless ones, without power it couldn't run for very long.

The office. He had that old-fashioned phone in his office. Surely that would work.

I fled through the stacks of books toward the back of the

store, moving as fast as I could in the dim light. The moon didn't help much back here, what little light there was threw strange shadows all around me, making everything look extra ominous.

When I came level with the alcove there was a loud bang from behind the door that led to Mr. Galinski's upstairs apartment. I yelped and bolted in the direction of the office, but before I got far there was a strange sliding, fluttering sound behind me and then a thump, like a single book falling off a shelf and then another and another. There was a grumbling roar and suddenly the bookshelf to my left gave a sort of shudder and lurch, and then it was falling toward me, books toppling from their places and slamming down on my head and shoulders.

I gave a sharp cry of fear and plunged down the hall toward the office just as an entire shelf came down behind me. There was a mighty crash and, without looking back I bolted inside the office and slammed the door behind me, shoving the lock into place with trembling fingers.

I fumbled for the old-fashioned phone on the desk and dialled the police, my heart hammering away in my chest.

"Hello," I cried, "help, there's been a murder."

"Name and location please," a crisp voice said.

"It's Jillian Harrington. I'm at the book store. At Cur…"

There was a sharp, crackling sound and then the line abruptly went dead.

## Chapter 9

$\mathcal{I}$ huddled under poor Mr. Galinski's desk, too afraid to even breathe let alone move. I kept the dead receiver clutched in my hand because even though there was no dial tone it still felt like some sort of lifeline to the outside world ... and maybe I could use it as a weapon if I had to.

Someone had bashed on the office door once and then there'd been the sound of more banging but further away. Wood cracked and splintered somewhere in the shop and then there was just silence.

After the crashing chaos of earlier, the quiet was somehow even more terrifying. I strained my ears into the darkness, imagining the murderer crouched somewhere in the darkness waiting for me. Was that the sound of footsteps just outside the door? Was that a key turning ever so quietly in the lock?

I heard the faint sound of glass breaking and maybe a cry of pain.

I couldn't tell what was real and what was my imagination anymore.

Finally, there really was a noise, the sound of many people

talking together and red and blue lights flashing across the walls.

*Oh, thank goodness*, I clambered to my feet nearly sobbing in relief and stumbled to the door of the office, still dragging the phone along with me, cord and all.

"In here," I called, scrabbling at the lock and throwing open the door, "I'm okay …"

There was shouting and I broke off in alarm just as I came face to face with a group of officers with their guns drawn. Before I could say a word, somebody tackled me from the side and threw me to the ground. Hard.

"Stay down," the man bellowed in my ear, "drop the gun. Drop it."

"Um, Billy," someone said, their voice muffled with what sounded suspiciously like laughter, "I don't think that's a gun."

There was silence, and then I felt the phone I'd been clutching being pried out of my hand and I was hauled unceremoniously to my feet.

"Billy Carmen?" I said incredulously, wondering who on earth had seen fit to give this man a gun and a uniform. He'd gone to school with Gil and I and, during the one semester he'd dated Kristal, he'd done his best to make my life as miserable as possible.

"Jillian Harrington?" he said, looking equally surprised. "What are you doing here?"

"Hiding from some psychopath," I said honestly. "Did you catch him? Have you called the ambulance yet? Mr. Galinski needs help."

"Yeah, sorry, he doesn't need an ambulance anymore."

I looked away, choking back a sob.

"He's really gone then?" I asked miserably, wiping at my eyes. "I mean, I saw the knife and everything but I hoped …"

I broke off when I saw the incredulous expression on Billy's face.

"What knife?" he asked, but just as I opened my mouth to confess that I'd recognized the Serpent's Blade another officer stepped in.

"Hey, Billy, you should come see this," he said.

"Yeah, in a minute, Carl. I'm a little busy here."

"Yeah, but ..."

"I said later," Billy snapped, glaring daggers at the younger officer. "I'm interviewing a prime suspect here."

"A suspect?" I said incredulously, "but surely you don't think ..."

"What were you doing here in the first place?" Billy demanded again.

"I ... I work here," I said shakily. "I called the police ... Mr. Galinski was ..." Here, I broke off and closed my eyes, tears running down my face.

"All right, all right, don't pass out on us. Come on, let's sit down. Layton, get her some water."

I reluctantly let him lead me down the hall toward the alcove but slid to a stop when I saw the door to the rare books room.

Deep gouges had been torn into the wood and the brass knob had been bent nearly in half. It had still held, though the killer had not been able to break through. It looked like someone had attacked it repeatedly with an axe.

Billy led me to one of the overstuffed leather couches. I sank into the deep seat and put my head in my hands.

"Here you are," a kindly voice said and I looked up to see a blonde female officer handing me a cup of water. She didn't look familiar, but at least she didn't seem as hostile as Billy did right now.

"Thank you," I said, taking the cup from her and drinking the whole thing in one go. I hadn't realized how thirsty I'd been.

*Where did all these police even come from?* I glanced past her out the office door at the officers swarming around in the book-store. When I was growing up, Maplegrove had only had one officer and a deputy. And there hadn't been enough crime to even warrant those two most of the time.

A strange, woozy feeling washed over me. How could any of this possibly be real? I must be in a dream somehow.

"Name?"

I jerked sharply back to reality to find Billy watching me suspiciously again, poised with a pen and paper in his hands.

I set the cup down carefully. "You know who I am, Billy. I'm Jillian Harrington. I live up at Greystone. I started working here for Mr. Galinski just a few days ago. Why are you asking me questions instead of—"

I stopped, remembering the way my former boss had stared so glassily up at the ceiling. This wasn't a dream.

"So, just to get this straight, what you're telling me is that you live up there in the lap of luxury and come here every day to this moldy old dump of a bookstore to work?"

"It's not a *dump*," I said, snapping my gaze up to meet his. He raised an eyebrow suspiciously and tapped his pen against the paper.

"It's a beautiful shop," I went on, ignoring the alarm bells inside my head that were telling me to shut up, "and I love books and Mr. Galinski was so kind …"

The officer's face blurred in front of me and I wiped a shaking hand across my eyes.

"Does your shift usually begin at three o'clock in the morn-ing?" he asked impatiently. "And do you usually show up looking like you're ready for the barnyard?"

"What?" I glanced down at my breeches, soaked from the knees down with poor Mr. Galinski's blood from when I'd knelt beside him. "Oh, yes. I start at nine normally, but today I …" I wondered for the first time how I was supposed to explain this part.

"Yes?" His voice was hard, suspicious.

"Well, I … I had a dream. Mr. Galinski was hurt and he was asking me to help."

There was a long pause.

"And you rushed all the way down here dressed like that on account of a dream?"

"It felt very real," I said haltingly, "and it scared me so I came right down. Mr. Galinski was … I thought he needed help."

"Hmm," the officer said and I felt his eyes boring holes in me. "So you're saying you got in your car and drove here in the middle of the night just like that."

"Oh, I didn't drive," I said before I could stop myself, "I rode my horse, Bally."

There was a long, tense silence. Probably the longest, tensest silence in the history of the universe. Billy made a little drawn-out snorting sound under his breath and raised his eyebrows, looking at me like I was completely nuts.

He had a point; there was little chance that the officer knew how bizarre a statement that really was since Bally was no longer living and all, but still, the fact that I'd gallop a horse all the way from home rather than drive sounded ridiculous, even to my ears.

"I see," he said finally. "And, just where is this horse of yours now?"

"Umm," I cleared my throat a few times. *Where was Bally, anyway?* "I sent him home?"

"All right," the officer said, pushing his chair back sharply. "I don't have time to sit here and sort out this mess. You're coming down to the station. You can give your statement there."

"Is there a problem here, Officer Carmen?" a cool voice said behind me, and Billy jerked upright, the supercilious expression disappearing completely off his face.

"Detective Anderson, Sir," he said, jumping to his feet. "You sure got here quickly. I was just questioning this witness here. I thought I'd save you some time."

"Very thoughtful of you. If you could go outside and make sure the perimeter of the crime scene stays secured, I would be very grateful."

"Yes, sir," Billy said and scurried off without a backward glance.

The Detective smiled at me and picked up Billy's notebook and read the notes slowly, only glancing up at me once.

"You came here because you had a dream?"

"I know it sounds so crazy," I sniffled, "but it seemed so real that I just had to come."

"I've heard stranger things, Miss Harrington," he said mildly. "I've known your family a long time."

I stared at him, wide-eyed, wondering what on earth *that* meant.

"What happened when you found the body?" He asked, raising an eyebrow.

I haltingly told him about trying to find the phone to get help for Mr. Galinski, and about the intruder who'd nearly killed me.

"Look," he said when I'd stuttered to a halt, "I don't think you had anything to do with your boss's murder, but your story doesn't exactly line up either. We're going to get you fingerprinted. Just a matter of procedure, that's all. After that, I'll send you home so I can continue my investigation, but I'll be coming around to talk to you in the morning. Does that sound fair?"

"Of course," I sniffled. Right then, all I wanted to do was go home, get into my bed, and stay there forever.

"Won't take a minute," a young sandy-haired officer said as he approached. He whipped out what looked like a small tablet.

I stared down dully as he rolled my fingers one by one across the screen.

"Not like the old ink and paper days, is it?" he asked with a smile. "With all this new technology out, it's a wonder anyone gets away with crime at all. You know I worked on this one case where——"

"Thank you, Officer Forelle, I'm sure you need to get back to work now. One thing, Miss Harrington, before you go; is there anyone you can think of who would have wanted to harm Mr. Galinski?"

"No." I shook my head. "Everyone loved him. I mean, yesterday was my first real day of work, but from what I saw he was respected in this community."

"He didn't mention being worried about break-ins or security? He didn't have anything valuable on the property that you know of?"

"Well, there is the rare books room," I said slowly, "and whoever broke in and killed him tried to get in that door. They wanted something, but I wouldn't know what anything is worth in there."

"Right, well, if there's nothing else then you can head home."

I headed toward the door again and then stopped. "His former assistant Toby might know more," I said, "I don't know if they've left town or not yet, but he worked here for a while before he was fired. His father was here yesterday to take him home. Toby might have a better idea than me of what things are worth."

"He was fired?"

"Uh, yes. He was caught stealing." I broke off. "But he's just a small teenager. There's no way he could have killed anyone or done all this damage."

"Huh, you'd be surprised. Any idea where he was staying?"

"No, I have no idea. His father said something about

packing him off to military school. They came to apologize to Mr. Galinski yesterday afternoon."

"Is there someone you can call to come and pick you up?" he said, changing the subject abruptly.

"Yes, I can call someone from the house. But I don't have my phone. I forgot it at home."

"Huh," he said thoughtfully, "I didn't think anyone let their phones out of their sight anymore these days. I'll see if I can round one up for you. Sit tight."

As soon as he was gone, I started to shiver. The shock of everything that had happened finally kicked in and I couldn't stop my teeth from chattering. I couldn't just sit there any longer.

I got to my feet and stepped further out into the now-ravaged bookstore. The first shelf that had nearly toppled on me had hit the shelf next to it, and the next, and they lay half-leaning on each other like fallen dominoes.

Books were scattered everywhere and I gazed in awe at the destruction. I hadn't heard more than one intruder, but it was amazing that one single person could have caused all this damage.

*Poor books*, I thought, seeing all the broken spines and torn pages.

I stood at the edge of the chaos, watching the police swarm around the room. Their flashlights cast strange shadows making everything seem twice as ominous. Thumps came from upstairs and I guessed they were searching Mr.Galinski's apartment.

*I should tell them about the hidden workshop*, I thought but hesitated. The killer wasn't in there and spilling all Mr. Galinski's secrets without thinking it through first wasn't going to help bring him back.

"Come on, let's get you outside to make that phone call,"

Officer Layton said, appearing beside me. "You don't need to see all this."

Detective Anderson looked up from where he knelt beside the body and gave us both a nod as we passed slowly by. A white sheet had been draped carefully over Mr. Galinski.

"On second thought, Officer Layton can just drive you home," he said, "we'll need to keep your clothes as evidence, though. You can hand them over to her once you're home and changed into something else."

I nodded, still feeling that this must be some horrible nightmare. My gaze drifted instinctively back to the body and I froze in my tracks.

*The sheet is flat*, I thought, my breath catching in my throat, *there's no knife sticking out of him. The Serpent's Blade is gone.*

So that's why Billy had been so weird when I'd mentioned the knife. There wasn't one.

"Hey, Detective Anderson," another young officer shone his flashlight carefully across the floor between the body and the broken glass by the front door. "Check this out."

The detective moved forward and I automatically followed. Between the body and the door were two human footprints outlined in blood and beside them were several strange circular marks. They looked just like hoof prints.

*Bally*, I thought, glancing around as if I'd find him hiding behind the cash register or something. *He must have been in here.*

"Pictures." Detective Anderson said swiftly. "Document everything carefully and someone look into getting power to this building. We can't do much in the dark."

"Come on," Officer Layton tugged gently on my sleeve and we went outside, skirting carefully around the crime scene.

The sky had lightened up to the palest shade of grey and a couple of the nearby businesses were just beginning to open their doors. The smell of fresh roasting coffee beans spilled over from MapleBrew and the light from the SapAndSuds laundromat across the road flicked on.

*It must be six o'clock then*, I thought blearily.

A couple of early morning dog-walkers had paused just outside the police tape and were watching the action in fascination. A few faces were pressed up against the coffee shop window and I recognized Kristal's blonde hair, but I couldn't tell if Katie was there, too.

"Are you taking her down to the station for more questioning?" Billy said maliciously, right next to my ear.

I jumped and moved away from his salami-scented breath.

Officer Layton raised her eyebrows and shook her head.

"I'm taking her home. The Detective will talk to her later."

"Home?" Billy said incredulously. "They might want to keep a closer eye on her than that. Rich people like that can just book a flight and disappear at a moment's notice. Her type will do anything to weasel out of trouble. I've seen how her family operates before."

*Huh?* I stared at him in astonishment. I had no idea what he was talking about or where this sudden bitterness had come from. But it most likely had something to do with my mother.

Before I could respond, a familiar blue truck screeched up to the curb and Gil leapt out onto the sidewalk. I was never so glad to see anyone in my entire life.

We moved at the same time, colliding together as he wrapped me in a bone-crushing hug and I buried my face in his jacket, clinging to him for dear life. Both our hearts were thudding and we stood frozen like that until Officer Layton cleared her throat behind me.

"Um," she said, "how about you guys go on ahead. I'll follow you in my car."

I nodded as Gil took my hand tightly and led me to the truck. To my surprise Christoph was in the driver's seat, his face pale in the early morning light.

"Thank goodness you're okay," he said as I squeezed in between them. "We were so worried."

"I'm okay, but poor Mr. Galinski isn't," I said, my voice trembling. I looked out the window and caught sight of Kristal, now with a few early morning customers, still standing by MapleBrew's huge window. She locked eyes with me and for once, she didn't have her face twisted in its signature sneer. Instead, she looked … frightened.

## Chapter 10

*T*he second the truck pulled away from the curb all the adrenaline left my body and I sank back into the leather seat and closed my eyes tightly. I slid down as far as I could to avoid the curious gazes of anyone who happened to be watching.

Gil squeezed my hand and Christoph reached out to pat my arm reassuringly.

"How did you know I was here?" I asked, not opening my eyes.

"Your mother," Christoph said after a long pause, "she called from Patagonia and was quite insistent that I get out of bed and find you. She said you were in trouble and that you were somewhere with books."

"Oh," I said, opening my eyes abruptly.

*Now, does she actually care what happens to me or was she just trying to avoid a scandal?*

"I called the house and woke up Betty. She said you weren't in bed and then Gil said—"

"I just remembered that you were working at the bookstore," Gil interrupted quickly. "It was a lucky guess."

I stared at him, wondering why the colour had risen in his cheeks and that he'd suddenly turned to stare out the window.

"Well, thanks for coming to get me anyway. And sorry Mother woke you up."

"Oh, don't worry about that," Christoph said dryly, "it wasn't the first time and I'm sure it won't be the last."

He laughed and shook his head. I wondered how much he knew about our family. Both he and Gil had been with us a long time. They must have seen some pretty weird stuff over the years.

Gil gave me a sideways look but said nothing, just squeezed my hand tighter.

When I got home, Morris greeted me at the kitchen door, meowing hard and rubbing up against my ankles as if I'd been gone for years rather than just a morning. Then Betty appeared, wrapping me in a tight hug.

"Oh my goodness," she said, staring at my bloodstained clothes in shock, "Jillian, change out of those awful things at once and have a hot bath. I'll make you some nice breakfast. You poor thing."

"I'd love a hot bath," I said, "but Officer Layton will be here any second and she'll want to take these with her. I'll run and change and then be right back."

I wearily trudged up the stairs, feeling like my legs could barely hold me upright. I peeled off the ruined breeches, gagging a little at the spots where the blood had soaked through and tinted my legs. I tossed everything in a pile while I rummaged around for clean clothes. There was no sign of either Nanny or Bally.

Officer Layton was in the kitchen tucking into a plate of eggs and bacon when I got back. Christoph and Gil were right beside her. Betty looked more than pleased to be feeding people again.

"Oh, put them in here," Officer Layton said around a

mouthful of food and pushed a gigantic clear Ziploc bag in my direction. "I'm afraid we'll need your coat and boots too. Don't worry, we'll get them back to you as soon as possible."

"Okay," I said slowly. I went to get my coat from the rack near the door when something gold dangling from the left front pocket caught my eye.

In all the chaos, I'd forgotten the key that Mr. Galinski had shoved into my hand. I pulled it out carefully, keeping my body angled between the coat and the table, and hung the thin chain quickly around my neck, tucking the key under my shirt.

Behind me, the officer was animatedly telling a story about an elderly resident who kept calling the police on a hungry raccoon that kept walking in through her cat door to eat her cat's food.

"Here you go," I said, setting the bulging Ziploc on the end of the table. "That's everything."

"Perfect. Well, I guess I should be getting back." She smiled at us all, but it seemed to me that she lingered a little longer when she looked at Gil and her eyes sparkled just a little bit extra. "Thanks for breakfast. Detective Anderson will probably give you a call or drop in today."

Gil and Christoph stood up, their chairs scraping backward noisily.

"We should get to the horses," Christoph said, "we'll take care of yours too, Jilly, while you get a bit of rest."

I was too tired to argue at that point. Gil reached out and squeezed my hand in passing, and when he let go, I wished that he was staying.

"Right, upstairs for a bath and a rest, and I'll bring you your food," Betty ordered and I wearily obeyed her orders.

Climbing the stairs for the second time felt like climbing a mountain, and it wasn't until I was almost to my room that I remembered a key part of the tragic events that morning.

I doubled back into the hall and walked slowly toward the

display case, feeling a cold chill roll across the back of my neck. It was there, nestled darkly on its cushion just like it always was.

For a split second, I thought there'd been a mistake, that I'd been wrong about seeing the knife in poor Mr. Galinski all along. But as I looked down at curved lines of the Serpent's Blade my heart sank. It was a fake, a clever replica, good enough to fool someone who was just passing by, but not good enough to fool anyone who'd lived with the knife her whole life.

*This wasn't a petty thief who stole the blade just to sell it for money. This was carefully planned out. They needed that particular knife for a reason. But why would they kill Mr. Galinski? For what purpose?*

I ran the water and dumped in about five times the recommended amount of bubbles, watching listlessly as the rose-scented foam filled the tub. It was bliss to finally climb into the steaming hot water and close my eyes, but I couldn't make my mind relax.

*The man who came after me at the bookstore wasn't a random burglar. He was looking for something in particular. I need to know who it was and what he was after at the bookstore. Mr. Galinski told me to protect the book. But which one?*

Also lingering was the fear that maybe the burglar *hadn't* found what he was looking for when he'd went on his murderous rampage. Maybe it hadn't even been at the bookstore at all. Maybe it was *here* at Greystone and he would try and come back and find it. The thought of meeting that madman again in my own house was too terrifying for words.

A floorboard creaked and I felt my whole body tense and then relax again as Morris bunted open the bathroom door and trotted inside, settling himself down on the bathmat next to the tub for a good grooming session.

"You're such a good cat," I told him, stifling a yawn. He looked up at me with wide, green eyes, blinked once and then went back to washing.

I stayed in the bath until the bubbles melted and the water

went cold, and then dragged myself out of the tub, found my pyjamas, and climbed wearily into bed. Morris tucked himself in beside me and fell into a rumbling, soothing purr.

My thoughts finally slowed and my eyelids drifted shut. I didn't even wake up when Betty came in with my breakfast.

## Chapter 11

*B*y the time I opened my eyes, it was early afternoon and the guilt of ignoring my horses for so long forced me out of bed and into clothes again.

The shock and terror of the morning were still with me, but it felt distant somehow. Like I was separated from my emotions by a thin veil. I think that was the only way I could function when the image of Mr. Galinski's blank gaze came back to me over and over again.

The sun was out in full force, but the temperature had plummeted, freezing everything and turning the snowy paths hard and slick. More than once I nearly lost my footing.

The horses looked up from their lunch hay as I came in, not upset at all that their morning routine had been disrupted. They probably didn't care where I'd been as long as *somebody* had remembered to feed them.

"I'm so sorry I neglected you guys," I said. Allison laid her ears back and made a snarly face in my direction because that's just the type of girl she was, but everyone else went back to eating. I went straight to Damascus's stall, slid inside and then wrapped my arms around his fluffy neck and buried my face into his sweet-smelling fur. I didn't cry, but I felt a bit of the tension inside of me loosen and I heaved a deep sigh.

Damascus let me hug him for about a minute before he'd had enough. He squirmed around and lifted his head as high as it could go, rolling one eye back at me as if to ask what the heck I was doing hanging off his neck. I laughed and let go, giving his shoulder a good scratch instead. He turned and nuzzled my pockets looking for the cookies I often kept there.

"All right, you guys, I might as well get you all exercised. It's not like I have a workplace to go to anymore …"

Fresh tears stung my eyes but I brushed them away impatiently. The best way for me not to dwell on what had happened was to keep myself too busy to think about it.

I lunged Serena, Lilo, and Lark, and then let Damascus and Allison take turns playing loose in the arena. I'd decided that it wasn't worth fighting with Allison anymore; if she needed to run to blow off steam then that's what I would let her do. No sense with both of us being miserable.

She wasn't nearly so awful as she had been on the first day I'd free-lunged her. She calmed down much more quickly, and by the end, she was actually listening to me and could canter around me calmly in a circle without taking off in a bucking fit every time I moved or blinked.

Someone had already cleaned my stalls but I added extra bedding and topped the water buckets, and generally made sure my charges were comfortable.

"I wish you all could get some time outside," I told them, "but it's just so slippery. Maybe I can talk to Christoph about buying a load of sand to make a safe path for you all to walk on. Not that Mother would probably ever approve of paying for something like that. It's still worth a try, though."

Even though the barn was light and airy, and we had an indoor arena to play in, I didn't like the idea of them not getting any sunshine and fresh air for the next few months of winter.

I had just determined to go find Christoph and ask him when the phone in my pocket suddenly rang. It was such a rare sound that it made me jump. Even when the phone *was* working, hardly anyone ever called me. The number wasn't one I recognized but, figuring that it might be the police, I reluctantly answered it.

"Jillian Harrington?" a brisk voice said.

"Yes, that's me." I gulped, not liking his official tone.

"This is Eddie Halville, with the law firm of Halville, Halville and Halville. I'm afraid I'm calling on official business."

"Official business … with me?"

"Yes, I'm Sid Galinski's lawyer. Before his *untimely* death this morning, Sid asked me to contact those people he'd included in his will. You, Miss Harrington, are one of those people."

"Me," I said in astonishment, "but why? He barely knew me."

"Indeed," the lawyer said, a heavy note of disapproval in his voice, "but for whatever reason, my client wanted to list you as a beneficiary. Do you have time to come down to my office today?"

Going back into town was the last thing I wanted to do, but I supposed that I owed it to Mr. Galinski to at least see why he'd included me in his will when he didn't know anything about me.

"Of course, if that's what you'd like. What time?"

"Could you be here in an hour? I'd like to get Sid's affairs in order as soon as possible. He was a good man …" he broke off, clearing his throat several times. "I trust you know where our office is?"

"I'm sorry, I don't remember …"

"Oh, I would have thought you would have memorized *all*

the locations of your family's holdings by now," he said in a biting tone, "we're five doors down from my brother's hardware store. I believe you raised our rents at nearly the same time."

"Sorry," I said, wincing. "I don't have anything to do with the rentals. Mother handles——"

"I'm sure she does. Anyway, five doors down from the hardware store. I'll see you soon." And with that, the line went dead.

*Great, another person who hates my family*, I thought glumly. Maybe it would be easier to just move and start over fresh in a new town where nobody knew my name.

I ran inside to get changed and then headed to my little car shed to see if Myrtle was in a good mood.

"Come on, girl," I said, patting Myrtle's dashboard encouragingly as I tried to turn the engine one more time. Instead of rumbling to life, there was just a rasping, grinding sound and a cloud of blue-grey smoke drifted up around her. Probably not a good sign.

I looked down at my watch and sighed in frustration. I was going to be late for my appointment with the lawyer. Myrtle clearly wasn't going to cooperate today so I would have to ask someone for a ride.

I shut the car-shed up again and trudged to the barn. Betty was busy helping Mrs. Hopps and the Dutch girls pull apart the kitchen so they could scrub behind all the appliances so I knew I shouldn't disturb her. I was hoping that one of the stable hands might be headed to town for a feed or lunch run.

No such luck. The barn was uncharacteristically empty. I poked my head into the tack room but it was vacant, too.

*Where on earth is everyone?* I wondered. I walked to the end of the aisle and stared out the open bay door into the snowy landscape beyond and suddenly the faint trace of music caught my ear. A thumping bass reverberated across the ground and it seemed to be coming from the sagging wooden house that was our main staff accommodation. A loud cheer suddenly went up and I hesitantly walked in that direction.

*Are they having a party in the middle of the day?* I thought as I drew closer and the music became louder. Of course, when Mother had been here there would never have been music allowed at any hour, and the grooms would have at least pretended to look busy when she was around.

By the time I got to the drooping front porch, I couldn't hear a thing over the noise.

*Maybe I should just go and see if Betty can drive me after all,* I thought, nearly losing my nerve. But just then the door flew open and Raoul burst out, carrying a laughing, shrieking Sonja in his arms. He ran down the two steps without noticing me and dumped her into the nearest snowbank and proceeded to cover her with snow.

"Stop, you idiot," she cried, still choking with laughter, "get me out of here."

"You lost the bet, this is what you get," he said, grinning wickedly. And suddenly they both caught sight of me standing there.

"Oh," Sonja said and Raoul hastily pulled her out of the snowbank and onto her feet, making a feeble attempt to brush away the worst of the snow. "Hello."

"Um, hello," I said awkwardly, shrinking a little under their curious stares. Laughter, warmth, and music poured out of the dilapidated house and suddenly I realized that I hadn't been over to this side of the property in *years*. Not since I was a kid. The smell of food grilling on the barbeque floated through the air and I sniffed appreciatively.

Sonja sent me a tentative half-smile, but all the mirth drained out of Raoul's expression and he stared at me coldly, crossing his arms over his chest. I noticed that he had a bruise on his left cheekbone and a dark circle around one eye.

"Oh, what happened?" I asked in surprise.

At first, I thought he wasn't going to answer. Then he cleared his throat. "That idiot filly Christoph insisted on having me ride nearly flipped over on me," he said finally.

"That's awful, I hope you're not too badly hurt. Which filly was it?"

"I have no idea," he shrugged and looked away. "A red one that's dumb as a post and…"

"Sorry, Jilly, we're having a bit of a staff party," Sonja interrupted, glancing pointedly at Raoul to keep him from speaking again. "Christoph thought it would cheer us up because the power in the kitchen went out again; don't worry, nothing caught on fire this time. Did you want to join us? We're grilling steaks on the barbeque for lunch."

*Christoph organized a party?* I thought in astonishment. *Fire in the kitchen?*

"I'm sorry, I didn't mean to interrupt. My car wouldn't start and I was hoping someone was making a run to town that I could tag along with. I'm late for an appointment."

Raoul snorted under his breath. "So you think one of us should miss lunch and drop everything to chauffer you into town?"

"No, that's not what I meant. I had no idea you were having a party in the middle of the day."

I broke off, hating how that had sounded. I felt a hot blush burn my cheeks. Of course, I didn't *know* there was a party because I hadn't been invited.

"Hey, Sonja," Gil called, stepping onto the porch, "I need a partner for cards. Are you up?"

I stared at him, astonished. He was dressed in jeans and my favourite wool sweater I'd bought him a few Christmases ago. He looked very, very comfortable there.

He caught sight of me and his eyes opened wide. "Jilly. What are you doing here? Is everything okay?"

"Um, yes, of course," I said, blushing harder than ever and feeling like a complete intruder. "I'm sorry, my car wouldn't start and I needed to go to town. I didn't mean to interrupt—"

"Of course not. Come on in and have lunch with us, and then I can run you in. I was just catching up with these guys and filling them in on my brush with Olympic glory. I didn't know you were awake yet or I would have come over."

"I … I can't. I'm sorry but I'm late."

"What the ice princess is saying is that you should drop everything and do her bidding," Raoul said rudely, abandoning Sonja and stomping past me up the front steps.

"Hey"—Gil reached out and laid a firm hand on Raoul's shoulder—"that's enough."

"Yeah, whatever," Raoul grumbled, "suit yourself."

"Just ignore him," Sonja said in exasperation when he was gone, "that's what *we* all do. Sorry, we didn't think to invite you. We weren't being mean; we sort of just forgot you were here."

That was so much better.

"No problem," I said as brightly as I could, willing my voice not to betray any trace of the hurt I felt. "You guys have a good time. I'm going to head out now."

"Wait, don't you need a ride?" Gil called.

"No, I'm all good. See you later." I strode purposefully toward the barn as fast as I could, eager to put the whole awkward encounter far behind me. I would just have to interrupt Betty and ask her for a ride. Or maybe there was time for me to call a taxi, I was sure I had enough cash stuffed in my change jar to pay for at least one way.

Gil caught up with me before I was even halfway down the barn aisle.

"Hey, wait up," he said, matching my stride easily. "Come on, I'll drive you."

"You really don't have to," I said stiffly.

"You're being stubborn, my truck is right here and it will

take ten minutes for me to run you in. Where are you going anyway?"

"It's a little complicated," I said, "but I'm going to the lawyer's office. Apparently, Mr. Galinski left me something in his will. But you don't have to…"

"He did *what*?" Gil opened the passenger side door of his truck and ushered me inside.

"I know, it's crazy, isn't it? He barely knew me, so I'm not sure what to think."

"All right then, let's go."

## Chapter 12

*T*he ice-lined trees were melting under the winter sun, dripping everywhere. Water ran in fast-moving rivulets from the melting snowbanks into the road.

"These roads are going to be deadly tonight once it freezes again," Gil said ominously.

I agreed with him, glad that Myrtle would get to stay safe at home that evening. Driving on re-frozen ice-lined streets wasn't any fun at all.

I slid down in my seat as we drew closer to town, clasping my hands together tightly in my lap. We were just a block away from the bookstore when I finally looked up and took in the grim scene once again.

Despite it being hours after the crime had taken place, the sidewalk was still full of curious onlookers. At a spot nearest the door, a few mourners had already begun to lay bouquets of flowers, splashes of brilliant colour against the slushy, grey sidewalk.

Tears welled in my eyes and I had to look away. "He was a wonderful man," I said quietly and Gil reached out and squeezed my hand, not letting go until he had to turn the corner to park in front of the lawyer's building. It was an immaculately kept Victorian house that had been converted into an office with a wide front porch that was topped with lacy, scalloped trim. Despite the beauty of the house, it did not look very inviting. The hair at the back of my neck prickled as I slowly pushed open the truck door and started up the walkway.

"Wait, Jilly, I'll come with you."

I was too nervous to argue. A sharp, bitter smell filled the air like burning rubber or chemicals, but I didn't see any smoke. The second I put my foot on the front steps the porch swing in the corner began to rock wildly back and forth.

*That's not Nanny*, I thought grimly. *I wonder how many angry ghosts would haunt a lawyer's office?*

Gil stopped beside me and stared at the swing in confusion. "Do you see that? It's moving on its own. There must be a strange cross-breeze there or something."

"Yeah, or something," I muttered, moving purposefully toward the door. I refused to look at the swing again.

A chime rang quietly as we pushed inside and a woman looked up from the desk. She wore narrow reading glasses that tapered to sharp points at the edges and had styled her mousy-brown hair in a complicated bee-hive arrangement on top of her head. Even though she wore a welcoming expression, a faint aura of disapproval hung over her as she surveyed the two of us.

"Well, Jillian Harrington, as I live and breathe," she said, flashing me an insincere, toothy smile. "I haven't seen you since the night of your engagement party. Shame about how that all ended, you must have been devastated. I don't blame you for hiding yourself away like a hermit after that fiasco."

"Right," I said, fishing around in my memory for her name, "well, I've been busy with the horses …"

"And now"—she cut me off, dropping her voice to a

hushed whisper and shooting a glance over her shoulder toward one of the closed office doors— "I hear you've gotten yourself mixed up in a *murder*."

The last word trilled out louder than the others and I saw a gleam of excitement in her eyes.

"Um, well …"

"Is it true that this is your second brush with death in less than a year?"

She looked at me fixedly like a cat about to pounce.

"Mrs. Moore," a voice said sharply, and we all jumped and turned to see a younger, clean-cut man stride out of the second office, frowning heavily. "Did you let my uncle know that his clients are here?"

"Not yet, dear. He's on the phone," she said in a sickly-sweet voice meant for a two-year-old. "I was just about to ask our guests to have a seat. I've known Miss Harrington since she was a skinny little girl in pigtails. She was always nosing around and asking questions like a snoopy little detective. We were just catching up on old times."

Her insincere smile became even more strained.

What on earth had I done to her to make her so nasty? I didn't remember her at all.

"No need to disturb your work," the man said brusquely, "they can wait in my office."

"If that's what you think is best, dear," she said, gritting her teeth a little, "though it's certainly not how we did things here when my father was in charge."

Making a little tut-tutting sound under her breath, she sent us a bright, malicious look. "But then you young folk are full of modern ideas."

Gil and I glanced at each other with eyebrows raised; there was a lot of tension happening at Halville, Halville and Halville.

The younger man quickly ushered us into a spacious office, shutting the heavy wooden door firmly once we were inside.

"I'm Lance Halville, by the way Have a seat," he said, waving a hand in the direction of the plump leather couch. "Coffee or tea?"

"Coffee, please," Gil and I said at the same time, shooting each other faint smiles. We'd shared an addiction to good coffee since we were teenagers and we both liked it the same way; no sugar and lots of cream.

"I have a fresh pot on. Sorry about that old dragon out in the lobby. She's awful and if I had my way, we would have gotten rid of her a long time ago. My uncle won't hear of it, though; she's been working here for years. It used to be her father's practice back in the dark ages before he died and my father took it over. I can tell you that when I take over, she'll be the first thing to go, along with these blasted paintings."

He pointed to the far wall where three alarming abstracts full of red, pink, and orange paint slashes hung side by side.

"Anyway, I'm sorry about what happened this morning, Miss Harrington, you must still be in shock."

"I am," I admitted, "it doesn't seem real right now."

"No, that's the way it is with trauma. The after-effects take a few days, sometimes weeks, to kick in. We were sorry to call you in so soon, but it was Mr. Galinski's wish that you be notified as soon as possible."

"Do you know why?" I asked. "I mean, I'd only worked for him for barely a day. I wouldn't have expected that was long enough for him to add me to his will. When did he make the change?"

"Ah, well, I don't expect we'll ever know his motivations, but I'm sure my uncle can—"

Just then the door opened and a short, grey-haired man wearing a harassed expression bustled inside, carrying a thick file of papers in both hands.

"Thank you, *Mrs. Moore*," he said over his shoulder in a determined voice, "no, we don't need you to take notes and we'd prefer not to be disturbed."

He shut the door firmly and then, after a moment's hesitation, he turned the lock with a sharp click.

"Sorry about that. She's a little too helpful for comfort sometimes. Good woman, though. Very organized. Eddie Halville, pleased to meet you."

He pulled up a rolling leather chair beside his nephew's and sat down, opening the file on the desk. "Let's not waste time then, shall we?"

He suddenly looked up and stared searchingly into my face. "A lawyer is supposed to remain neutral at all times, Miss Harrington. I'm to follow my client's wishes to the letter without letting my personal feelings affect my duties. But in this case …"

He looked down and shook his head. "Sid Galinski was not just a client; he was a good friend. He was a kind and caring man. He was generous to a fault sometimes, and there were a few people who tried to take advantage of his good nature. Miss Harrington … if I was to find out that someone had ended that good man's life in order to benefit from a hastily amended will, I would be most disappointed. I really can't say what I'd *do* in that case, but I would make sure that justice was swift and severe."

"Now, wait a second," Gil cut in, "you can't think that Jilly had anything to do with the murder."

"I'm not the police or a judge," the lawyer said solemnly, "so I can't say that as yet."

"I didn't kill him," I said quietly. "I hadn't known him long but I agree with everything you said. Everyone loved him, he was a kind man. He gave me a chance when nobody else would, and I would have never done a thing to hurt him. I promise you I did *not* kill him."

We stared at each other in silence and then Mr. Halville sighed heavily. "I hope, for all our sakes, that you're telling the truth."

"Of course she is," Gil interrupted. "Besides, what on earth is in that will worth killing for? Did he leave Jilly a rare book collection or something?"

"He left her all of it," the lawyer said simply.

"All of what?" I asked in confusion.

"The entire bookstore, including inventory, the apartment above it and a sizeable amount of money."

"No," I said in astonishment. "That's impossible."

"I'm afraid it's very possible. Here, I'll read you the document in its entirety."

I sat there, still numb with astonishment, while the lawyer read the entire will to Gil and me. Mr. Galinski had truly left me everything, or at least his assets in MapleGrove, and I was now the owner of a bookstore and in possession of more personal money than I'd ever had in my life.

"Of course, you can't take full possession until the police investigation is done. Nobody is allowed to trespass on an active crime scene."

When I nodded he cleared his throat and went on.

"It will be at least a week or two, I'm afraid. The forensic experts are still going over it and then, of course, a clean-up crew will need to go in and sanitize the, er, crime scene before you can re-open. That will be on your dime, I'm afraid. I can organize that if you like."

"Yes, thank you," I said faintly, remembering with a sudden lurch of nausea the blood pooling on the wooden floor.

I didn't understand why any of this had happened, but I did know that Mr. Galinski's will had provided me with two things; a chance to protect the book he was talking about... and a very strong motive for his murder.

## Chapter 13

*E*verything was a blur after that. I barely heard anything else the lawyers said and I just signed the papers in front of me in a daze, hardly knowing what I was doing.

I was given a ring of keys to the shop and the apartment above and on the way out, the senior Mr. Halville had pushed a manila envelope into my hand.

"Mr. Galinski left you a letter, my dear. I was instructed to tell you to read it in private." He shot a stern look at Gil. "Alone."

I nodded and clutched the envelope all the way back to Greystone. So many thoughts were swirling through my head that I could hardly breathe.

"Let's get you inside," Gil said, sliding out of the truck after me.

But I stopped him before we reached the front door.

"I'm sorry, I need some time alone to process all this. Thanks for driving me. I'll see you later."

I saw the flash of hurt surprise on his face. But I didn't even hear his reply as I stumbled up the steps and into the house. As soon as I was inside, I fled upstairs and locked myself in my room.

I flung myself down on the bed beside a heavily sleeping Morris and held the envelope with shaking fingers. My name was written on the front of it in spidery handwriting, and I turned it over to find it stamped on the back with a small symbol. The circle inside a triangle, inside a square, inside a larger circle.

*That's the same symbol on that old book of Mr. Galinski's.*

A shiver ran down my neck and spine, and I looked up hoping that it was a familiar ghost and not a new one.

"Nanny?" I glanced over at her rocking chair but it was empty. Both she and Bally had been gone all day and I didn't like it. I could have used some advice about this whole thing and Nanny was pretty much the only one I could tell the whole story to without having to censor out the ghost parts.

*Well, here goes.* I tore open the envelope and pulled out the single sheet of paper. The first thing I noticed was the date in the upper right-hand corner.

*No, that can't be right,* I thought, *this is from over a year ago. He didn't even know me then.*

There were just a few paragraphs, but I smiled as I felt the warmth and kindness Mr. Galinski had put into them.

*Dearest girl,* it read, *if you are reading these words then my time on this earth has passed and I have moved on to the next grand adventure.*

*It must seem peculiar that I, a stranger, am leaving you my earthly treasures, but you will discover that the lives of our two families have been entwined one way or another for over two hundred years. I have watched you grow up, though you might not have realized it, and know of no better person to protect my secrets.*

*I know that the Way of the Alchemist is not yours, but you will be the one to pass the mantle on when the time is right. I know you will recognize my successor and do the right thing.*

*Greystone has always guarded its secrets and I know that you will be able to guard mine as well.*

There was a break in the writing and the next few lines had been heavily crossed out with a black marker. What replaced it was a hurried scrawl, still recognizable as his handwriting but written in a much different mood. Words had been scratched out here and there and a blob of ink smeared in the middle. It was dated from yesterday afternoon.

*Jillian, I have been a blind fool and I have run out of time. Take my precious collection to Greystone and keep it safe, destroy the cursed blade, hide the page, protect the book with your life. There are evil forces at play here. Trust no one. Destroy the blade. Good luck and sorry.*

He'd scrawled his signature in bold and finished the letter with that little stamped symbol again. The circle in the triangle, in the square inside the circle.

*What. The. Heck.*

I sat the letter down and looked around, half expecting someone to leap out and tell me this was a colossal joke and that I was being pranked.

I was startled out of my thoughts by a loud thundering sound downstairs. Morris leapt to his feet, jumped nimbly to the floor and trotted toward my bedroom door.

The sound came again and I stood up. Someone was using the awful brass lion-head knocker on the front door that sent the sound echoing through the far reaches of the house.

I looked at the letter and then reached down and stuffed it under my pillow to keep it from prying eyes.

"Coming," I said out loud, trotting down the stairs as fast as I could.

I threw open the front door and found Detective Anderson there standing with his back to me surveying the estate with an incredulous expression.

"Ah, Jillian Harrington," he said turning to face me, "we meet again. This is quite the spread you have here. I haven't been up here in many years. I'd forgotten how… impressive it is."

"Oh, thanks. Greystone's been in my family for a long time. Please come in."

He followed me inside and then stopped and looked around in wonder, whistling low under his breath.

"Miss Harrington," he said suddenly, "I dropped by earlier but was told you'd gone into town. I thought I told you to stay home."

"Um, you said to stick around. I just ran into Maplegrove for … some errands."

"Did those errands happen to have anything to do with suddenly inheriting a large sum of money?"

"Erm … yes," I said in resignation. It sure didn't take long for news to travel around here. "Did Mr. Halville call you already?"

"His secretary," the detective said dryly, "she was quite eager to inform us of your new inheritance."

"I didn't know anything about it beforehand," I said quickly. "I swear."

"Maybe. But you understand it doesn't look very good."

"I know, I know. But there isn't much I can do about that. It's just as much a surprise to me."

"Well, for now, we have another suspect. That's what I came up here to tell you. Or rather, warn you. That teenager, the former assistant you told us about, is missing and his father said that he took an important artifact with him when he disappeared."

"Toby," I said in surprise, "are you sure he hasn't been kidnapped or anything? What if he's in danger too?"

"His father doesn't seem to think so. The man was quite … insistent that we find the boy. He felt that he'd run away and taken some treasure or another to pawn for drugs. He said his son had fallen in with a bad crowd. He'd been kicked out of school last year after breaking into a display and stealing something. Apparently, he already had a bit of a record before he moved here."

I thought about the sad, defeated-looking boy I'd seen the other day and shook my head. Maybe I was just naïve, but I didn't think him capable of murder.

"What did he say his son took?" I asked slowly.

"Some sort of rare knife with a snake figure on it. Apparently, there are only a handful of them in the world and they're quite valuable to collectors. You said you saw a knife when you first found the body, was there anything serpent-like about it?"

I hesitated.

*Destroy the blade*, Mr. Galinski's note had read, he must have meant The Serpent's Blade. How was it all connected, though?

"Miss Harrington?"

"It was very dark," I said finally. "It was hard to tell, but I suppose there might have been something carved on the hilt."

"Very good. Well, we'll find the boy soon enough. We sent out an APB and half the countryside will be looking for him soon. Still, you should keep your doors locked and let me know if you see anything strange. This house has a lot of valuables in it and if the boy is still in the area, he might be desperate enough to try and steal something else."

"Oh, right, thanks," I said, attempting to answer his smile while my thoughts were still a million miles away. "I will."

"That's a nice cat you have there," he said, pointing at Morris who was now lying on his back in the middle of the hall with his paws in the air. "You might consider upgrading to a dog though. My sister volunteers at the Greenville Animal Shelter. She could probably find something for you. A dog that can guard the house but also be a companion. I heard that your family is out of the country for the time being. With everything going on here, it's not ideal that you're all alone in the house."

"Oh, I'm not alone," I said quickly. "We have, er, staff here."

"Ah, yes." He cleared his throat. "Not quite the same as a family though, is it?"

"I… I suppose not." Though that wasn't exactly true. Betty, Gil and Christoph were more like family to me than my own parents, honestly. But as for the rest of the staff…. I couldn't see them going out of their way to protect me from a burglar.

"Well, think about it. The shelter just got in a litter of puppies and they have older dogs as well. All shapes and sizes. We'll be in touch."

I watched him as he got back in the car and headed down the driveway.

"Don't worry, Morris, I won't upgrade you," I said, quietly. Although the idea of getting a dog was tempting. I'd always wanted one.

The big cat looked at me languidly and blinked once, utterly certain of his top position in the house.

There was a shimmer in the air outside and then Bally appeared, standing partway down the driveway, staring at me pointedly.

"You're back," I called happily, glad I could put at least one of my worries aside. It wasn't like him to be gone this long, but maybe transporting me from home to town in the way he'd done had drained him of energy or something. "Hang on, I'll be right there."

I shut the front door and hurried to the side kitchen where my boots and jacket were kept. Betty had hung up some of my old things to replace the clothing I'd had to give to the police. Nothing would clear my head better than a walk right now.

The sun was bright and the air was warm, and if I hadn't felt so hollow still it would have been a beautiful day. Bally nickered as I got close and I smiled at the familiar sound. He rubbed my shoulder with his nose and the slight jostle made the chain around my neck shift a little and I suddenly remembered the key Mr. Galinski had given me. The key he'd pressed into my hand and begged me to take.

"Come on boy, let's go." We trekked through the sunshine, up past our usual lookout spot and out onto the snowy, rolling pastures beyond. I hadn't been to the woods in a long time and I needed to move to wear off some of the nervous energy churning through me.

Bally made a little snorting sound and then broke into a trot, heading toward a figure who was coming out of the trees.

Gil couldn't see the horse, of course, but the pensive look on his face fell away and he lifted a hand in greeting.

"Jilly," he called, "What are you doing way out here?"

"Same as you, just going for a walk. Why are you out here?

"Just thinking, I guess."

Bally was following closely behind Gil, a person he'd adored while he was alive, and I wished so badly that Gil could see him. I was beyond tempted to just tell him the entire truth. There was a small chance that he wouldn't believe me, that he'd think I was crazy. But I didn't think so.

Which only left the roadblock of me trying to protect him from danger.

.  .  .

"So, what did the letter from Mr. Galinski say? Did he explain why he wanted to leave you the store?"

"Um, sort of." I hesitated, wondering how much I should share. "Well, he wanted one thing from me anyway. There was a book that was important to him, one he'd shown me the other day at work. In the letter, he asked me to protect it."

"Protect it? From what?"

"The murderer tried hard to break down the door to the rare books room. I'm almost certain now that he was after that book. I have no idea why, but something in there must be important. I suppose it could just be worth a lot of money."

"Did you tell the police that?"

"Not yet, I haven't had time to sort everything out in my head yet and besides, Detective Anderson came by and said they're pretty sure Mr. Galinski's old assistant Toby robbed the store and murdered him for drug money or something."

"But you don't think so?"

"I'm not sure, honestly. I don't know if a teenager could have done all that damage. Toby didn't seem very … athletic."

"People on drugs are capable of doing some crazy stuff, though."

"True, and there could have been more than one of them. It was dark and I was scared; it could have been anyone in there."

We climbed in silence for a few minutes.

"I was thinking that maybe I could go back to the store and see if the book is still there at least. I could make sure it hasn't been stolen."

"The lawyer said you wouldn't be allowed in for a few weeks, though."

"Well … yes," I said slowly, "but I was just thinking…"

"No."

"What?"

"Whatever you're thinking. No. Just let the police do their

job, Jilly. There might be a murderer loose. They have an officer posted at the bookshop. Nobody is going to break in. You'll just have to wait until they say you can go in."

"But the book—"

"Will still be there in two weeks. It's not worth breaking in and getting arrested or worse, running into some drug-addicted thief. Right?"

"Hmm," I said non-committedly. "You *could* be right. Hey, you never told me the details about how Coconut did in training. Is he on his way to being an Olympic horse?"

Gil looked at me suspiciously but let me change the subject.

I half-listened to his story about life with an Olympian, but the other half of me was thinking about the book.

*Mr. Galinski wanted me to have this key for a reason*, I thought, *he trusted me to protect the book. I owe it to him to at least try.*

Up ahead, Bally flicked his tail and snorted as if he could read my thoughts.

No, I definitely couldn't wait a week or two until the police cleared me to get into the bookstore. The rare books room door had been hacked up pretty good, who knew if it could withstand another attack if the killer showed up again. The book might be in danger. I had to get back in there. Tonight.

## Chapter 14

*I*t wasn't the brightest idea I'd ever had, but the more I thought about it the more logical it seemed. Which is how I found myself all dressed in black, sitting alone in a freezing car in the middle of the night feeling very much like a criminal.

*It's not like I'm even breaking in*, I reminded myself as I peered through Myrtle's smudged front window into the darkness, *I own the building now. I have a key. I'll just have to find a way to get past that idiot Billy to use it.*

I didn't know what Billy had done to be demoted to standing on guard duty in front of Curiosity in the bitter cold, but I was glad it was him and not someone smarter.

I'd eased Myrtle into a spot behind a couple of parked cars, three blocks down in front of Bark n' Stuff which was the local pet and feed store. It was as far away as I could get and still be able to see Curiosity's front door. I'd been there for over an hour and so far, Billy hadn't moved more than a few feet away from his post. Right now, he was hopping up and down under the streetlight, stomping his boots against the ground, probably in an effort to thaw his frozen toes.

The temperature had dropped steadily in the last few hours and, as predicted, everything that had melted in the daytime had now turned to solid ice. Even wrapped in warm thermal layers and wearing a fluffy coat, I was beginning to feel uncomfortably cold.

The town was asleep, all the businesses had shut down hours ago, and only MapleBrew had a dim light glowing from some unseen back room. Someone must be in there finishing up paperwork or preparing baked goods for the next day.

*I'll never get in through the front of the store*, I thought grimly. *Billy isn't going anywhere soon and that streetlamp lights everything up like Christmas. I'll have to sneak around back somehow and try the service door.*

I'd sat still long enough; it was time for action. Just in case Billy had eagle-eye vision that I didn't know about, I slid across the seat and exited Myrtle from the passenger side door. Creeping out and staying low until I was safe in the shadows. Then I hurried up the street in the opposite direction from the bookstore, turning right and going another two blocks before turning again. I didn't know this part of town well. I spent most of my time on the farm and I hadn't had many reasons to go into the residential section of MapleGrove before.

The streetlights were further apart here, but even in the semi-darkness, I could see that the houses were mostly beautiful old renovated Victorians, much like the lawyer's office, with tidy front yards and wide front porches.

A few lights were on, but most of the houses were in darkness; bedtime came early in the winter in Maplegrove.

I counted three and a half blocks and then slowed my pace. If I followed this next street, I would eventually find myself at the corner where MapleBrew and Curiosity sat across the road from one another. I was crossing my fingers that the bookstore didn't have a guard posted to the back as well. My best plan was to hide behind the coffee shop for a few minutes so I could scout things out.

There were very few streetlights on this secluded section of road so I was easily able to whisk up the street unseen and tuck myself in under the metal staircase that led up to the area above MapleBrew.

*I wonder if anyone lives up there?* I thought, glancing anxiously upwards into the darkness. There was a tiny glow from inside but for all I knew it was just a reflection of a clock or something.

The last thing I needed was a nosy neighbour to find me skulking in a back alley across from the crime scene.

From my hiding spot, I could only see the side profile of the bookstore. The streetlight lit up the huge picture window near the front with its display of books still neatly arranged inside. I'd handled those books just a few days ago but it seemed like a lifetime away. A few unbidden tears stung my eyes as I thought about the loss of Mr. Galinski.

*I will find this book for you*, I vowed, *I will find out who did this to you, too.*

Greystone's blade had been used to kill a good man. I owed it to him to find out the truth.

The night grew even colder and I decided that I needed to make my move soon before I turned into a popsicle. Permanently.

I couldn't see Billy from my position. He must be tucked right under the awning by the door. I was just about ready to finally make my move when there was a scuffling sound behind me and someone cleared their throat in the darkness.

I spun around, cursing myself for not bringing some sort of weapon, and found Katie standing a few feet away. She was dressed in black from head to toe like I was and was glaring at me with a fierce expression.

"Shh," she said fiercely as I yelped in surprise. "He'll hear you."

I put a hand over my wildly beating heart and leaned against the brick wall of the building. I really was not cut out for this espionage thing.

"Katie?" I said in astonishment. "What are you doing here?"

"I work here, remember? What are you doing here?"

"Um, well …" I hesitated. There probably wasn't any great explanation as to why I was lurking in the darkness. "I'm trying to get into the bookstore."

"Yeah, I guessed that. But why?"

"Mr. Galinski left me the store in his will," I admitted, deciding that honesty was the easiest plan of action.

"He did?" she asked in shock. "But why?"

"I have no idea, but he wanted me to get something for him. To keep it safe. I need to get in there to find it."

"So, like, does that mean you have a key?"

I paused before answering, taking in her pale, tight-lipped expression. She hadn't been innocently loitering outside of the coffee shop. She was a girl on a mission.

"I do have a key. What are you *really* doing here, Katie?" I asked her gently and to my surprise, she abruptly dissolved into tears. She didn't make a sound, just sobbed quietly with one hand over her mouth and the other over her eyes as if to block me from seeing her.

"They … that detective thinks Toby was the murderer," she said finally. "But it's not true. He would have never hurt anyone. I wanted to prove …"

She wiped her sleeve across her face and sniffed.

"I just wanted to find some evidence to prove he's innocent, that's all."

"Look," I whispered after a long pause, "I agree with you. I was in the shop just after it happened and I don't think a small teenager could have caused all that destruction. Not alone anyway."

"So, you believe me? Really?" She looked up, her red-rimmed eyes shining with hope. "Nobody else does. Aunt Kristal hated when I hung out with Toby."

"She did? Why?"

Katie shrugged. "I don't know. He made a mistake one time and stole something. But, I mean, like it was one time. And he apologized for it and everything. She just didn't like him, I guess. Either way, I want to go with you."

"Katie, it might be dangerous and it's a school night. What will your mom say if you're out this late?"

"She doesn't care what I do," Katie said quickly. "I'm not even at home this week anyway. Aunt Kristal lets me stay upstairs in the shop when my home-life gets … complicated.

"We're wasting time talking, though. That stupid guard told me earlier that he'll change shifts in an hour. We should have about forty-five minutes to get in and out again before a fresh cop comes on duty. Come on, someone might see us if we cross the road here, I have a better plan."

She disappeared into the darkness in the opposite direction of the bookstore motioning at me to follow.

After a moment, I sighed and followed her into the night. It wasn't like I had a better idea anyway.

We went back up the block and down a whole other street before doubling back into the alley that ran behind the shops from the other direction. I didn't know if it had been strictly necessary, but we *had* managed to avoid the streetlights. We arrived at the bookstore without incident and paused in the inky darkness to listen for the guard. I was suddenly thankful that Katie was there with me and I was not doing this all on my own.

"I think it's all clear," she whispered, "do you have the key?"

I pulled the ring of keys from my pocket and tried them one by one. I heard Katie huff impatiently as I fumbled in the darkness.

*Let her try doing this by feel, without a light, with half-frozen fingers,* I thought grumpily as the third key slipped from my grasp. But finally, I found the right one, the lock clicked and the big door swung silently open.

We both froze. There was the slimmest of chances that Billy had gone inside and was waiting there for us in the darkness. But after a moment of nothing happening, we slid silently into the bookstore. I shut the door quietly behind us and drew the lock shut again.

The light from the streetlamp outside flooded in and I could see that everything was still in chaos just as I'd left it. The shelves lay fallen atop one another and books were scattered everywhere, their pages splayed open, spines bent. It made me ill just to look at it again. It was as if the whole tableau had been frozen in time; I half-expected poor Mr. Galinski to still be lying there on the floor by the cash register.

*If only I could go back in time. If only I could have been there an hour earlier. I might have been able to help him.*

Pushing away my dark thoughts, I headed past the fallen shelves directly toward the rare book room. I was almost certain I'd find the old book there. That was my first destination, and then I'd try out the laboratory next if we still had time.

"Whoa," Katie breathed as she caught sight of the still-locked door in the dim shadows. It looked like it had been attacked with a blunt axe. Hack marks and gouges scored the whole upper side of the door and the ornate handle had been nearly bashed in half.

"Wow, that's crazy. Can you still get in?" Katie hissed next to my ear.

"I don't know." I fished for the chain on my neck and

leaned down so I could use the key without having to take off the necklace. To my surprise, after a bit of fumbling, the key turned easily in the lock and I was able to jiggle what was left of the handle carefully open. The battered door swung inward with only the faintest of groans.

"If we shut the door, we should be able to use a flashlight," Katie whispered, pulling the door closed behind us.

We held our breath as her light flicked on, illuminating the little room. It was peacefully undisturbed; at least one part of the bookstore hadn't been harmed in the murderous rampage. It made me feel slightly better that at least a little of what was important to Mr. Galinski had gone undamaged. It felt like a little part of him, maybe the most important part, had survived.

"What are we looking for?" Katie whispered, but I didn't answer.

I flicked on my flashlight and shone it carefully around the room. The place was full of ancient, crumbling books and it took me a minute to find what I was looking for. He hadn't hidden it. The book was sitting right on the back counter in plain sight. He must have trusted that this room was impenetrable or maybe he'd just thought he'd have more time.

I recognized the peeling leather cover with the strange symbol embossed onto it right away. On impulse I opened it carefully and peered down at the illustrations in front of me without touching the crumbling paper, studying the faded, brown ink with a feeling of sorrow. How could this old book be important enough to kill for?

"We'll look around to see if there's anything else important," I said, unzipping the front of my coat and putting the book inside against my sweater before zipping it up again. "But I'm taking this with me."

It was bulky, but if were suddenly discovered I wanted a chance to be able to escape with it safely.

We searched the room from top to bottom. But without knowing what we were looking for it was impossible to tell which books were the most important. And we were running out of time. I looked around the room swiftly, wondering if there was anything else I should take.

"Come on, let's get out of here," Katie said finally, "there's nothing in here but books. I want to find some proof as to who killed Mr. G."

"Like what?" I asked but she shrugged and turned away without answering.

She flicked her flashlight off and I slowly opened the door inch by inch, pausing often to listen intently into the darkness. Nothing moved and we crept carefully out of the little room. I pushed the door shut again and made sure it was locked tight. The lock probably wouldn't hold up to another attack but at least it would slow the thief down.

*I promise I'll get the rest of your collection safely to Greystone as fast as I can*, I thought, sending my intention out to Mr. Galinski, wherever he was.

"I just have to look at one more thing in the office," I whispered to Katie.

She nodded and followed me closely. This part of the hall was almost completely in darkness, but it was too exposed for us to use flashlights; Billy would see the beams easily. It wasn't until I opened the door to the office that the moonlight found us again.

Mr. Galinski's desk looked just how I'd left it. A little messy but otherwise undisturbed.

*I guess I'll have to do this in front of Katie*, I thought uncomfortably, but it wasn't like I could send her away without either endangering her or risking us getting caught. And it wasn't like I was going to keep the laboratory going once I took possession of Curiosity, either. I had no intention of being an alchemist or finding any elixir to make people live forever.

"Whoa," Katie said again when the filing cabinet swung open to reveal the little workshop beyond. "So, this is what he meant."

"Who?" I asked but she was looking beyond me with wide eyes like she hadn't heard me.

She flicked the flashlight on and my heart sank. Everything had been destroyed. The glass tubes had been smashed and the whirring machine lay on the floor with its inner wires ripped out. Shattered glass lay everywhere, and I could see that liquid from the vials had dripped everywhere, leaving half-congealed puddles of goo on every surface.

"Don't touch anything," I said quickly. "I have no idea what chemicals he was working with."

"What on earth was he doing, though?" Katie asked.

"It's a long story," I said, "but I don't think it was anything bad. He was a good man."

Katie sent me an intense look that I couldn't interpret in the dim light but it felt almost angry.

"Let's get out of here," she said finally, "we're out of time."

I followed her back through the store, stepping over the fallen books and shelves again with a pang of regret. I couldn't wait to get back in here and clean everything up.

We didn't say another word until we'd cleared the back door and were halfway up the street.

"Well, I guess I'd better head home," I said, "you have school tomorrow and I have a whole lot of research to do."

"You think that the book will help you solve the murder?"

"I don't know, maybe. I hope so."

"And you'll tell me for sure if you find anything?"

"I will. If I find anything that helps you figure out if Toby is involved. You don't know where he ran away to, do you?"

We were nearing where I'd parked Myrtle when a dark shadow stepped out from behind a tree nearly scaring me half to death.

"Hello, Jilly," a familiar voice, now laced with anger, said. "What exactly do you think you're doing out here?"

Katie and I both yelped with surprise and Katie bolted up the street a few feet before turning around again.

"Gil," I said, gasping for breath. "You nearly gave me a heart attack. What are you doing out here?"

"Looking for you," he said shortly. "Why didn't you answer your phone?"

"My… oh, I had it turned off," I said guiltily. I hadn't wanted it to ring while I was inside Curiosity so I'd turned it off before I left home. "I'm sorry. Were you trying to reach me?"

"We left you dozens of messages. The whole farm thinks you're missing and someone broke into the house again."

"No!" I gasped. "That's impossible. Why?"

"I don't know," he said grimly, "but a few of the display cases were broken and the archive room has been torn apart. I think some artifacts are missing. Someone was looking for something."

"Goodnight, Katie," I said hurriedly. "I'll be in touch."

"But … I can help," Katie protested. "This might be another clue."

"Not this time, I'll call you in the next few days."

Katie looked at me sulkily for a moment and then turned on her heel and strode away into the darkness without saying another word.

"I'll follow you home," Gil said shortly, moving toward the truck he'd parked behind Myrtle.

"Gil," I said, "I was just …"

"Please don't tell me that you were breaking into the book-store to find that book—"

"I have a key," I protested, "and I was just —"

"Yeah, I know, heading straight toward danger," he said gruffly. "Again. I'll see you at home."

There was a tense moment there where I wasn't sure if Myrtle would start or not, but she finally choked to life and, after a few minutes of running to let her thaw out and defrost her windows, I headed back to Greystone with Gil following closely behind.

"I don't know why he always gets so angry with me," I muttered out loud, glancing back in my rear-view mirror.

"Because he loves you, dear," Nanny said from the seat beside me and I jerked the wheel, nearly careening off the road.

"Nanny, don't *do* that. Especially while I'm driving."

"Tut, tut, no need to be so jumpy. Are you taking a multivitamin every day like I told you? It might help calm your nerves."

"Multivitamin? Nanny, I'm in the middle of a murder investigation. I don't think vitamins are going to cut it."

"A healthy diet leads to a clear mind and a strong body. If you're going to be running from desperate killers then you'll need to be both physically and mentally fit."

"I hope to *never* be running from desperate killers," I said emphatically. "I just want to figure out who murdered Mr. Galinski and stole the blade so I can turn the evidence over to the police and *they* can do the running."

"Hmph," Nanny said, "that doesn't sound very adventurous. Where's the fun in that?"

I shook my head and sighed. Maybe running from danger sounded fun to a ghost who couldn't actually *die* a second time, but I did not find it appealing at all. I'd had way more than my share of adventure this year and I wondered when the peaceful, quiet life I'd wished for was going to materialize again.

"Anyway, you're changing the subject, my girl, why are you causing that man back there a world of grief when he loves you so much? He's trying to help and you're shutting him out."

"Oh, Nanny," I sighed. "I don't know if he loves me in the

way you're thinking. He cares for me, he feels sorry for me, and he's spent his whole life trying to protect me. It's probably just an old habit by now. Honestly, I think he deserves to do something better with his life than trying to contain my disasters."

"Jillian Laurel Harrington, that is the stupidest thing I think I've ever heard you say," Nanny said in astonishment.

"It isn't stupid," I said sharply, "Gil has said it before. I'm like a magnet for trouble. And murder, apparently. What if my gift comes back full force and I have all sorts of ghosts asking me to help them? I don't know how dangerous that is going to be.

I can't ask him to commit to a lifetime of that, Nanny. He could find a nice, simple girl and have a safe, normal life. Besides, Gil is the most honest person I know, and if I let him in on our family secrets then it will be the same as asking him to lie for the rest of his life. He'll always be living a double life. That's not fair to ask of him. I don't know why you can't see that."

"Don't you use that tone with me, young lady," Nanny said huffily, "Well, I can see that you don't need any of my advice since you know everything. If you'll excuse me, I have some knitting to catch up on."

"Wait, Nanny, I didn't mean—"

But she'd already disappeared.

"Great," I muttered. "That went well."

A few minutes later, I pulled up in front of the manor with Gil right behind me. Four police cars were parked in front of the house, and beside them sat an ambulance, all their lights whirling, sending splashes of colour across Greystone's exterior.

It seemed like everyone who lived on the estate, both house and stable staff, was crowded around on the lawn outside. The majority were huddled around a lone figure near the ambulance and as I drew closer, I realized that Betty was at the center and that an EMT was just putting a bandage on her forehead.

"What's going on?" I asked, feeling a stab of panic as I rushed to Betty's side. "What happened?"

Betty was the toughest person I knew, and her pale face and frightened eyes scared me more than anything.

"Oh, Jilly, thank goodness you're all right. I was so worried," she said reaching out to clasp my hand.

"Forget about me, what happened to you?"

"I don't know," she said. "One minute I was coming home through the kitchen door, and the next moment I heard a noise, and before I could turn around someone grabbed me from behind and then hit me. I woke up on the floor. I didn't know where you were. I thought you'd been kidnapped."

"I'm so sorry," I said, stricken with guilt. "I shouldn't have left like that without saying where I was going. I didn't mean to worry you. I shouldn't have turned my phone off."

"I'm all right, dear, they just need to take me to the hospital for the night for observation."

"Nothing to be worried about," the EMT said kindly, "but she took a pretty good knock to the head. We worry about concussions, especially in older…" He clamped his mouth shut, catching Betty's glare. "Anyway, we'll have her right as rain by tomorrow, I'm sure. You can probably pick her up in the afternoon."

Everyone hugged Betty as she was loaded into the ambulance, calling out well-wishes as she was driven away. The Dutch girls began to cry and Mrs. Hopps reluctantly patted their shoulders a few times to reassure them.

"The police are searching the house right now," Gil said to me quietly so nobody could overhear. "Detective Anderson was looking for you specifically. Do you want them to find the book?"

"No," I whispered back. "I need to keep it a secret for now."

"Give it to me. I'll hide it and then you won't be lying if they happen to ask about it."

I didn't think anyone but the killer would ask about the old book, but I didn't see any easy way to sneak it into the house right now.

"I promise to tell you all about it later," I said and I meant it. It was getting too hard to keep all this to myself. I needed help.

Facing the truck, I unzipped my jacket and handed the book to Gil who zipped it into his own parka. He disappeared without a word and I forced myself to not watch him leave.

"Jillian Harrington," Detective Anderson said from behind me, "how nice of you to show up."

I opened my mouth to tell him my quickly made-up story of how I'd just dropped into town to talk to Katie about riding the horses, but he held up his hand to stop me.

"We'll be sure to take a full statement later. Right now, I need help getting everyone organized. The staff will need to be fingerprinted and the rest of the property searched. I need a list of other houses, barns, and outbuildings where a person might hide. This doesn't have the makings of a normal break and enter. They were looking for something specific. I need you to verify if anything is missing."

"Okay," I said meekly. "I'll help you however I can."

"The old guy said there's no security system and no cameras," a brown-haired man said, pointing over his shoulder to a glowering Mr. Hopps. "They really live in the dark ages here. They don't even have a dog."

They both turned to stare at me and I shrugged. Greystone had always seemed an impenetrable fortress to me, but I guessed that it could use a little updating. I had a feeling the security system and the cameras wouldn't work very well, but there was that dog idea again …

*I suppose nobody would have ever dared to break in when Mother was here full-time*, I thought ruefully, *her reputation probably terrified everyone away. I'm going to have to work on my intimidation skills.*

"Come inside then," the detective said, and I followed him into the house, worried about what I'd find there.

The door hung open but the kitchen looked pretty much normal. The coat rack had been knocked askew but other than that, it had been undisturbed.

The hall beyond was full of people. Officers moved up and down the stairs, talking in low voices. A man marched by carrying a hard silver briefcase in one hand, a large duffle bag thrown over one shoulder. He trotted up the stairs without saying a word.

"Come on upstairs, I'll show you where the most obvious damage was done first. You certainly keep a lot of valuables on-site for people who don't have a security system."

"Well, lots of things here are old but not worth much money. Many only have sentimental value to our family. And it's not as easy to sell stolen art and museum pieces as you'd think. The antiquities community is not that big, and most people would rather turn a thief in than risk buying stolen goods."

"You seem to know an awful lot about it," the detective said over his shoulder.

"Mother," I said as if that was enough of an explanation. "She loves collecting things and she used to drag me around to different shows and sales, so I know more than I want to."

He smiled and then stopped in front of the ruined display case that up until yesterday had housed the Serpent's Blade.

In truth, it had most recently housed the *fake* Serpent's Blade. So why had it been stolen now? Who would have bothered to break in and steal a fake knife a day after the real one was stolen?

*Someone who didn't know the real one had been taken,* I thought, looking anxiously at the shattered glass and deep grooves in the base. The thief hadn't known enough to just lift the glass lid away either; instead, they'd smashed it and dented the base in the process. It was a very violent and crude way to do things and I gave a little shudder.

"That was the Serpent's Blade," I told the detective. "An old family heirloom originally brought from India. There were only five made, all by the same artist back in the sixteen hundreds …"

My thoughts whirled. It was my ancestor, Gregory, who was supposed to have brought this back on one of his journeys. I wasn't sure exactly the timeline on that, but what if it was the dark relic he'd brought back to help him with the alchemy. The one Mr. Galinski said he and August had fought over.

I shook my head and brought myself back to the present to find Detective Anderson staring at me curiously.

"I noticed none of the other displays have been disturbed, just this one. It looks like the thief was after that specific knife. Now, I believe you have a sort of treasure room that was the next target."

"Treasure room? Oh, you mean the artifacts room off the library. Darn it, I hope they didn't destroy anything. Some of that stuff is ancient."

"Miss Harrington, I hope you're aware that most people do not have an artifacts room in their homes."

I wasn't actually, but then I didn't go to many people's homes. And when I *did* get invited to visit somewhere new, I was too busy trying not to seem outwardly weird or awkward to worry about where they put their collections.

I held my breath as we went in through the library and entered the little room where my parents kept the older collections that weren't quite nice enough to display. At first, I thought my worst fears were confirmed. Drawers had been spilled open and dumped everywhere and the glass over my father's antique coin collection had been cracked. But when I looked closer, I could see that the damage was probably not that bad.

"I have no idea if anything is missing. I'd have to go through it all and probably ask my parents. I haven't been in here in months."

We walked back into the library and I stood in place, rotating slowly to see if anything had been damaged or stolen.

"Anything?" the detective asked, watching my face closely.

I shook my head and then stopped. The black book that my ancestor Alocious had written wasn't where I'd left it.

*Mrs. Hopps probably just put it away when she was cleaning in here,* I told myself, trying not to feel any panic. That was not a book I wanted out in the world somewhere. Mother would be furious if it fell into the wrong hands.

"Jillian?"

"I'm not sure. I think I left a book out on that end table but it's gone now. Someone could have put it back on one of the shelves, though."

"Was it valuable?"

"I don't think so, but it's been handed down in my family for generations."

We did a walk-through of the rest of the house, but as far as I could tell none of the other rooms had been disturbed.

After that, there wasn't much for me to do. The detective had enlisted Mrs. Hopps's help to round up all the barn staff and the Dutch girls, and poor Mr. Hopps, who was still in his housecoat. Everyone was escorted to the library to be set up for fingerprints. The officers asked some basic questions while they waited, like where the staff had been when the knife was stolen and where they were at the time when poor Mr. Galinski had been killed.

The fingerprinting had provoked a lot of interest on everyone's part and the Dutch girls whipped out their cell phones so they could have selfies taken of themselves getting printed.

I parked myself in an overstuffed chair and was half-asleep by the time they'd roused me to go to the barn.

Everyone else had been sent home, but the detective said he wanted me with him to point out any items that might be missing.

"Nice barn," Detective Anderson said when I flicked on the lights. "So, which horse did you say you rode to town on?"

I was overtired and the question was so casual that I had to stop myself just in time from answering it truthfully.

"Um ..." I looked down the aisle of horses, frozen with indecision.

Suddenly, Allison put her big head over her stall door and gave a hearty snort in our direction. She pinned her ears flat against her head and gave the detective a nasty look, causing him to take a few prudent steps backward.

"Allison," I said firmly, crossing my fingers behind my back.

"Er"—he looked at the mare in alarm as she bared her teeth at him. "And how did she get home?"

"She must have found her way back on her own," I said, hoping this sounded plausible to a non-horse person.

"Horses have a good sense of direction," Gil said from behind me. I hadn't even heard him coming down the stairs. "If you turn them loose, they will usually find their way back to their homes."

"Is that right? Well, that's a fact I did not know." Detective Anderson scribbled something on his notepad and looked back and forth between us both. "So, a horse can run, let's see, ten or fifteen kilometers to town and back again without any ill effects, can they?"

"If they're fit, they can," Gil said, shooting me a sideways look when the detective turned away again.

"I see. Well, she certainly looks healthy enough. I suppose if nothing is missing then I'll move on to the staff quarters."

There had been a bit of grumbling back at the manor when the grooms found out that the police wanted to search their house. But nobody cared enough to make the detective come back with a warrant.

"I haven't done laundry in a week," Sonja complained, "my room's going to smell to high-heaven just so you know."

"I consider myself warned," the detective said, suppressing a smile. "And you, young man," he called sharply, just as Raoul was about to slink out a side door. "If you could wait here while we search that would be very helpful."

Raoul sent him a dark look and threw himself down full-length on one of the couches and pretended to fall asleep.

I yawned and rubbed my eyes as we started toward the staff house, wondering when this night would finally be over. All I wanted to do was sleep for about a century.

"Jilly, go upstairs to my place and rest for a while," Gil said kindly. "I'll come and get you when they're done or if the detective needs you. You look dead on your feet."

I resisted for about a millisecond before taking him up on his offer and climbing tiredly up the worn stairs to his apartment above the barn.

Originally, the suite had been where Christoph and the then eight-year-old Gil had lived when they'd first arrived at the farm. Later on, Mother had moved them into the nice brick house that had once belonged to the long-deceased gardener's family and they'd lived there for years until Gil had grown up and needed more space of his own. Then he had moved into the suite above the barn again.

As a child, I'd spent half my time hanging out either up in

the loft or over at Gil and Christoph's house but, as a teenager and an adult, I'd stopped going over there almost completely.

It was a cozy space. Just a big open room that held a living room, dining room, and a kitchen with a large bank of windows along one wall and bookshelves completely taking up the other wall. The space was surprisingly tidy; the hardwood floor and oak tables were a bit dusty but everything else was neatly arranged.

I sank down on the leather couch and pulled the fleece blanket from the back around me, yawning uncontrollably. There was something about this space that made me feel warm and secure, like I could relax and just let the worries of the past few months, and especially the last day, drift away.

I closed my eyes and fell into a deep, dreamless, sleep.

## Chapter 15

"*R*ise and shine sleepyhead, there's coffee to drink and chores to be done."

"Whaaaaa?" I blinked my eyes in the dim light and sat up, pushing the mound of blankets off me. A pile of warm covers had been added to the fleece I'd snuggled up with and I'd somehow gained a pillow and a large, orange tabby cat in the process.

"Morris," I said affectionately, rubbing his ears as he rumbled into full purr-mode." What are you doing here? What time is it?"

"Eleven o 'clock," Gil said, handing me a steaming cup of coffee.

"But it can't be, it's light out," I said in confusion, gratefully taking the cup and inhaling the earthy aroma.

"Eleven in the morning, Jilly," he said with a laugh, "you slept through the entire night."

"No way," I said in shock. "I couldn't have. My poor horses."

"Don't worry, we took care of them. You looked like you needed the rest. You must have been exhausted."

"Thank you, I was. I haven't slept like that in years."

I looked around instinctively for Bally, but he was nowhere to be seen. I frowned, hoping that he hadn't missed me last night. Would he even know to find me here?

"Breakfast is almost ready," Gil said, breaking through my train of thought, and for the first time, I realized that the air was full of the most delicious smells. Eggs cooking, bacon frying, and bread getting nice and crisp in the toaster.

"Oh, you don't have to cook for me. Let me help."

"No, no, you just sit there and drink your coffee. You're my guest today."

I sank back gratefully into the cushions and drew Morris into my lap, suddenly feeling a little shy to be in Gilbert's loft while he cooked breakfast for me. It was a bit too close to the future I sometimes imagined for myself when I was feeling sentimental.

"Here you go, madam," he said teasingly, handing me my plate.

I took it eagerly from him and tucked my legs up underneath me on the couch so Gil could share the space beside me. Morris kneaded the blankets in delight, thrilled that there were not one but two plates of bacon so close to his twitching whiskers.

"He's not much of a barn cat anymore," Gil said laughing. "You've spoiled him."

"That's my father's doing, not mine," I laughed. "They were getting along just great before dad was whisked away to Patagonia. Morris loved him. I don't think Dad's ever been able to have a pet before."

"You sound like you miss him."

"I do. It's sort of always been the two of us against Mother's tyranny and it's … well, it's lonely over there on my own. Betty has her own life, and Mrs. Hopps and the Dutch girls go home the second the housework is done. If it weren't for

Nan…" I was suddenly aware of what I'd been about to say and bit into a mouthful of egg so I'd stop talking.

*Will I ever get better about keeping secrets?* I wondered. *No wonder Mother never wanted anyone but family around. It's exhausting to have to pretend all the time. And this is what I'd be asking Gil to do too if I let him into this world.*

Gil looked at me closely and took a careful bite of his own food.

"Jilly," he said finally, "you're my best friend and I love you. I want to help you with whatever it is you're going through. But you're going to have to be honest with me if you want me to stick around."

"Honest about what?" I said nervously.

"Lots of things, but for starters, why did you break into Mr. Galinski's book shop last night?"

Oh, thank goodness he'd picked an easy one.

"I'll show you," I said, glad it wasn't going to be anything difficult like explaining ghosts. "Is the book still safe?"

"Right there," he said, pointing at the table next to the couch.

I sighed in relief when I saw the book unharmed. "Where did you hide it?"

"Allison's stall. I figured nobody would want to look in there."

"You've got that right." I laughed. "Okay, I'll tell you what I know."

As he finished the rest of his breakfast, I told him everything that had happened on my first day of work. I told him about the book and the secret lab, and about meeting Toby and his father. And I told him about Mr. Galinski's ancestor Simon and how he was connected to my family history. I told him everything except what involved ghosts.

"Wow," he said when I was finished. "How do you get yourself involved with these crazy things?"

I shrugged. "I'm not sure. But now I have a book and no knife. Mr. Galinski said to protect the book and destroy the blade. And I have no idea why he wanted me to do either of those things. Maybe he was just going a little crazy."

"I don't know, someone was obsessive enough to kill him for some reason. It must be all connected. So, your alchemy book was what August was using to help him create the so-called Elixir of Life?"

"Yes, I think so. That's the theory anyway."

"And you think that his brother Gregory brought the Serpent's Blade home from India to speed up the work somehow. Then he and his brother fought and August ended up dead. Drowned and with a knife in his chest."

"Yeah, probably not just any knife, though. I need to do a bit more research on that. But I think maybe August was killed the same way Mr. Galinski was, with the Serpent's Blade."

"And you said the knife was a bit weird, right, because it had that chamber for poison in it, too?"

"It's supposed to be hollow right from the tip to the hilt, to the spot where the poison is stored. But I don't know why that part is so special when it's just as easy to stab someone outright. Who needs poison?"

"Good point. Well, let's do some more research after our chores are done. We'll figure it out somehow. I don't want you going off on your own again. Especially not back to the bookstore, it's not safe right now."

"Fine," I said, agreeing easily since I had no intention of putting myself into danger for at least a week. I needed a good, solid vacation from dodging murderers.

"So, one more thing," he said mildly, catching me off guard. "What's this nonsense about you riding a horse to town the other day? I can't believe you lied to that detective."

I sputtered on my coffee and swallowed hard, coughing

and choking a little longer than necessary to buy some time. I should have known there was no way he'd let that go.

"Erm, that part I can't exactly tell you," I finally wheezed. I wasn't willing to lie outright to Gil. For one thing, I cared about him too much to be dishonest, and for another, we'd known each other so long that he could catch me in a lie before I'd even opened my mouth.

"You didn't ride Allison. She was asleep in her stall when I came downstairs that morning."

"No, I didn't ride Allison."

"So, someone drove you then. You got a lift in a car."

I shook my head and pressed my lips together. "No."

"You're really not going to tell me. You're going to make me drag it out of you?"

"Stop, Gil," I said, "you know I'd tell you if I could."

"That's bull, Jilly. You're choosing to shut me out and you know it. Look, I'm not blind and I know Bally's death hit you hard. But whatever *this* is, these so-called secrets you think you have to keep, has to stop. It's not healthy and it's causing you to push everyone away."

Tears welled in my eyes and I looked away.

*Tell him*, a voice inside urged, and I took a deep, steadying breath, looking for the right words to explain.

Suddenly, there was a clomping, scraping sound from the kitchen and I looked up to find Bally calmly eating the leftover egg from the frying pan, his teeth grinding across the metal.

Despite the seriousness of the conversation, I had to smile. He was so proud of himself for finding a perfectly good snack just lying around.

Gil frowned and looked up, his gaze following mine toward the stove. For a moment his eyes widened, and then he shook his head and looked back at me again.

"Jilly, are you listening to me?"

"Um, yes, of course, I am," I said, watching as Bally moved

from the frying pan to the basket of apples that Gil kept at one end of the counter. His nose twitched appreciatively and he flapped his lips as he drew nearer to the basket. I forced myself to look away and pay attention to what Gil was saying.

"… I think we need to take down Bally's nameplate and clean out that stall so that you can move on."

"Oh, no, he'd hate that," I said involuntarily.

Gil's eyes widened and he just stared at me, a troubled look on his face.

"Jilly," he said finally. but right then he was interrupted by the entire apple basket tumbling to the floor, apples bouncing across the room in all directions.

Gil jerked in surprise but I, of course, was already laughing at the sight of Bally eagerly pouncing on a rolling apple and disappearing into thin air.

"Sorry," I said, getting up to collect the fallen fruit from the far corners of the kitchen.

"Why should you be sorry? They're *my* apples," Gil said, laughing despite his confusion. "I must have set the basket too close to the edge of the counter. Or maybe I have mice."

"That must be it," I said, suppressing a smile. "Mice. Big ones."

We grinned at each other and then Gil reached out swiftly and pulled me into a tight hug.

"Life with you is never boring, Jilly," he said, kissing me on the top of my head.

"Maybe you'd like boring," I mumbled into his shirt. "Or at least *normal.*"

"Oh, I don't know." I felt his laugh reverberate in his chest. "Normal is probably overrated."

"It would be nice to at least try it. Even once," I said with a sigh.

"Come on, let's get our horses exercised and then we can

go over this book you were so set on stealing. We can take a rain check on the normal."

I reluctantly let him go, relieved that the earlier tension between us had disappeared.

"You know you're kind of a great guy, sometimes," I told him. And though my voice was teasing, the meaning behind it was serious. Gil had always been there for me, something I'd have to remember not to take for granted.

"Sometimes? You mean all the time. Let's go. Those horses won't exercise themselves."

We walked down the steps together and I couldn't help but notice that Gilbert's tiny loft felt way more like home to me than the manor ever had.

## Chapter 16

The first thing I did was go back to the house and change since I was still wearing my book-stealing outfit from the night before.

Greystone felt different this morning, like a stranger full of secrets instead of an old friend. Mrs. Hopps and her helpers had cleaned up most of the mess on the landing, but the smashed display case was a stark reminder that I was no longer completely safe in my own home.

I avoided looking at any more of the damage and hurried to my room, checking first under my pillow for Mr. Galinski's letter.

To my relief, it was still there and I read it quickly one more time, memorizing the words before throwing it into the smouldering fireplace.

*I'll have to be careful from now on,* I told myself while I watched it burn to ash. *That could have fallen into the wrong hands.*

I showered quickly and then pulled on breeches and a sweater before hurrying back outside.

Mr. Galinski was still on my mind as I worked my horses one by one.

Gil had his hand's full riding a bunch of youngsters under the careful eye of Christoph so I concentrated on ground work with my guys.

By mid-morning, the drifts outside had melted into piles of slush again and it was safe enough to get my horses outside for real walks.

"Enjoy it while you can," I told Serena as I hand-walked her around the farm, "this chinook weather won't last much longer and then we'll be back to raging winter again."

The horses appreciated the time outside; their eyes brightened and their steps quickened as they eagerly sniffed the morning air.

I had to wait until the ring was free so I could let Allison free for a good play session. She needed to be a bit tired out before I risked bringing her outside. Otherwise, I could just envision her bolting away and dragging me through the snow behind her.

Bally frolicked happily around outside the barn the whole time, setting even the quietest horses to prancing when he flew by kicking his heels in the air.

"Do you have to do that?" I said out loud, as I backed a snorting, pawing Damascus up a few steps to remind him that he was not allowed to charge off with his friend when I was attached to him by his halter and lead-rope, no matter how excited he was.

Bally shook his head and did one final buck and then settled down with a contented snort of his own.

By the time my stalls were done and all the horses were exercised and tucked in with fresh hay and water, my stomach was grumbling with hunger.

"Let's eat at your house," Gil said when he caught up with me. "I'm pretty much out of food at my place."

"Sure, I need to start cleaning up some of that mess too and seeing if anything else is missing. I felt bad leaving the house unguarded last night, but I'm glad I didn't have to sleep there alone, either."

We made a simple lunch of grilled cheese and soup together and ate at the kitchen table with the book spread out in front of us.

"Half these words aren't even in English," I said as we turned the pages carefully and studied the complicated illustrations. Some pages were filled with writing, but others were a mixture of arcane symbols and figures. Some had more complex ink drawings of scenery, people, or animals. The only thing the pages seemed to have in common was that none of them made any sense.

Mr. Galinski had spent his whole life studying alchemy in general, and this book specifically. There was probably little hope that we'd be able to piece much together in a few hours.

"Hey, look at this," Gil said.

I'd stopped to rub my tired eyes but when I looked up again, I saw he'd flipped to the very back of the book where one of the thick pages had been roughly torn out. The jagged edge looked fresh too, the white tear standing out against the rest of the yellowed pages.

"Find the page," I said, shock rippling through me as I remembered Mr. Galinski's final words.

"What?"

"When he died, Mr. Galinski told me to protect the book, find the page and destroy the blade. This must be the page he was talking about."

"Do you think this is what Toby tried to steal from him?" Gil asked slowly.

"Maybe. Possibly. It was something from the rare book room, though, and I don't think he would have fired him unless it was something important."

Something caught my eye and I tugged the book toward me.

"Hey, Gil check this out, there's an imprint on the back cover."

He leaned forward and then got up to turn on the overhead kitchen light so we could see better. We bent over it, our heads nearly touching, just barely able to make out the faintest of figures that had been impressed on the inside back cover of the book.

"We need paper and pencils," Gil said suddenly, "I know how we can find out what it said."

I fled to the office and scrounged around in my father's desk until I found a stack of blank paper and a handful of pencils.

"Here," I said, handing the papers to Gil.

He laid two of them next to one another on the back cover of the book and then picked up a pencil and began to rub the side of the lead gently across the page from one side to the other. At first, nothing happened and then gradually the missing image was revealed.

"Whoa, what the heck is that?" I whispered, feeling the hairs on the back of my neck rise.

In the upper left-hand corner was a pretty clear sketch of a now-familiar-looking knife.

*The damned Serpent's Blade*, I thought, my heart sinking.

The next image showed a couple of stick figures hugging.

*Aw, well, that's not so bad.* I leaned forward a little more. Darn it, on closer inspection they weren't hugging at all. One of the little figures was stabbing the other in the chest.

"Um, what sort of stuff did you say Mr. Galinski was into?" Gil asked quietly, stilling his pencil.

"Not this … whatever *this* is," I said quickly, "he said very specifically that a true student of alchemy took a sort of spiritual path that transcended the quest for gold or immortality. He said that anyone who tried to hurry the process through dark means could never truly be an alchemist."

The series of images revealed themselves a little like the panes in a comic strip, one by one. There was the dead stick figure, knife still in his chest, lying beside some sort of table full of equipment. Then the same figure again, this time with two hourglasses beside him. Then the next image was a close-up of the knife itself being immersed in some sort of liquid. Then just a series of words and symbols I couldn't understand. The last symbol was the same as the one on the front of the book and on the letter Mr. Galinski had left me.

"These don't fit in with the rest of the book very well, do they?" I asked. "The writing and figures are completely different. Like they were added later."

We stared down at the gruesome tableau without saying a word.

"Do you think the person stabbed was supposed to be given everlasting life by the Serpent's Blade?" Gil asked slowly.

I thought about it and shook my head. "Maybe. But August didn't come back to life and neither did Mr. Galinski."

"Oh, no." I put a hand over my mouth, trying not to gag at the unpleasant realization that had struck me cold.

"What? What is it?"

"Gil, I don't think the groove in the blade was meant to hold poison." My hands trembled as I ran them over the pencil rubbing again. "What if it was for blood? What if it drew the blood *out* of its victims so it could be used in the alchemy process somehow?"

"I wonder," he said slowly. "How can we be sure though?"

"We can't. But maybe this page is a sort of manual for something. Those hourglasses there might have shown how long the knife was supposed to stay in the body. Maybe the blood was changed somehow inside the knife's chamber. When the blade was removed the, er, contents could be used in whatever stage happened next in creating the Elixir of Life."

"That's a horrific thought."

My thoughts whirled as I tried to piece the whole thing together. "So, maybe Toby steals this piece of paper so he can make the Elixir himself. Then he breaks in here to steal the Serpent's Blade and replace it with a fake. Then he breaks into Mr. Galinski's store, kills him, leaves the blade in long enough to get the blood, and then goes on a rampage looking for the book?"

"But then he's interrupted by you, and then the police, so he has to pull the knife early and escape with it. But he still needed the book. He probably couldn't find it at the bookstore so he broke in here because he assumed that Mr. Galinski had given it to you."

I nodded slowly, frowning.

"Some pieces fit, I guess. But why would he then steal back the fake Serpent's Blade that he put here earlier? It just doesn't make sense. And I really can't see a kid doing all those things."

"You only met him for a minute. It's pretty hard to judge him in such a short time."

"I guess, but I just have a feeling …"

A cool breeze blew across my cheek and my skin prickled. I felt a little tug on my fingers and smelled the faint odour of lavender and old books wafting over me.

*Library-ghost.* I resisted for a moment but the next tug was much harder so I slowly rose to my feet.

"Jilly? What's wrong? Where are you going?"

"I just have to check out something in the library," I said vaguely as I felt the tug again. "I'll be right back."

Before I could stop him, Gil got up and followed me.

To my surprise, she didn't lead me to the library as I'd expected, she went straight to my father's office instead, tugging my fingers every time I hesitated.

*Okay, okay, I'm coming*, I thought at her but she didn't slow down.

We pushed into the office and the papers on the desk fluttered a little as if a window had been opened.

*There?* I wondered and headed toward the desk. The papers fluttered again and I looked down. There was a pile of spreadsheets in one corner, lists of stocks and hundreds of numbers beside them. Both my parents enjoyed playing the stock market heavily and they weren't bothered that my mother's pre-cognitive skills allowed them to come out on top more often than not.

*Just hoarding treasure like dragons,* I thought, rolling my eyes.

I laid my hand on the stack, wondering what I should be looking at when a splash of grey near the bottom of the pile caught my eye. I moved the spreadsheets aside and uncovered part of a folded newspaper trapped underneath. It was dated from about six months ago.

"What is it?" Gil asked, coming up close behind me.

"I'm not sure exactly," I said, scanning the page. None of the headlines seemed to have anything to do with us. But finally, a tiny blurb near the bottom caught my eye.

*Student Charged with School Break-In.*

The photo below showed a wooden display case with a hole smashed in the front.

*A young student was recently charged with breaking into his own school to steal a rare knife from a travelling museum exhibit. The government-sponsored program seeks to introduce high school students to some of the mysterious wonders of the ancient world.*

*"They're actually all replicas," the exhibit manager assured reporters, "we honestly wouldn't trust these kids with the real objects."*

*The would-be thief seemed to have missed that announcement. When questioned, the boy said he did it as part of a dare. His reward: expulsion from school and criminal charges. Although surveillance cameras caught the boy red-handed, the knife was never recovered and he insisted that the item had been destroyed.*

*The boy's father, a professor of antiquities, agreed to pay for all damages.*

"So that's where the fake knife came from," I said sadly. "I suppose that Toby is guilty of everything after all. Poor Katie, she really believes he's innocent."

"Jilly," Gil said, and I realized that he'd been staring at me incredulously the whole time. "How did you know this was here?"

I stared back at him, at a loss for words. Now was the time to tell him but my hands trembled where I held the newspaper and a cold sweat broke out across my forehead. I was so not ready for this.

"Gil, I see… I mean I *have* a sort of intuition," I said, stumbling over the words. "Sometimes I just get these, ah, nudges, to do something…"

The smell of lavender grew stronger and the paper in my hand fluttered lightly. I couldn't tell if she approved or disapproved of my half-truths.

"And if I follow them then it often leads me to discover answers to my questions."

I swallowed hard, trying to read Gil's expression. He knew me well enough to guess that I wasn't sharing the whole truth but I hoped that my compromise would be enough.

"Really?" Gil said, arms folded across his chest and eyebrows raised. "Intuition?"

"It's the best way to explain it right now," I said, setting the paper down on the desk and wiping my sweating palms together.

He was silent for a moment and then he sighed and nodded.

"Alright, I'll buy that. For now. But why was this paper on your parent's desk?"

That was a very good question. Was it just a coincidence or something to do with my mother's precognition? How would she know to keep a vital piece of the puzzle we were working on when it appeared six months ago in a newspaper from across the country?

I really hoped I wasn't going to have to call her and find out.

## Chapter 17

Christoph called to tell us that when he'd arrived at the hospital to pick up Betty that they'd told him they needed to keep her for another two nights just to monitor her.

"Oh, poor Betty. And we didn't even visit her. I was sure she was coming home today."

I vowed to visit her as soon as I was able tomorrow.

It was getting dark by the time we headed back outside to do night feed. Normally I tried to avoid this time of day because I knew the barn would be full of the other workers.

Voices rang in the air, horses neighed and the radio was blaring. Everyone was busy, some feeding, some still tacking up or cooling down their horses. It was a situation I usually managed to avoid; I always held off working my horses until there were as few people as possible around.

I hurried to take care of my horses and then helped Gil by finishing cleaning his stalls while he took Coconut out to stretch his legs in the ring.

"Ah, there's our little criminal," Raoul sang out as he sauntered toward me. The bruise over his eye had turned from blue to yellow, giving him a sallow expression.

"Lay off," Sonja said sharply, sending him a look. "She's been through a lot in the last few days, don't you think?"

"What I *think* is that you should let me ride that mare of yours," he said, pointing a finger at Allison, who responded by flattening her ears and wrinkling her nose at him in a horsey snarl. "You're not doing anything with her anyway. You're just letting her go to waste."

"She's not being wasted," I said, feeling my temper rise. "I exercise her every day. She's happy enough."

"She's an athlete," he said, echoing the words Christoph had said to me earlier in the week, "and she deserves a rider who can handle her … not some little girl who's afraid to even get on her back."

"Is that what you think?" I said in astonishment. It hadn't even crossed my mind that anyone would think I was afraid to ride. But I supposed that it might seem that way to someone like Raoul, who had probably never grieved for a dead horse in his life, didn't know me and had never seen me ride.

I glanced over at Bally's empty stall and then back at Allison. Her ears popped forward and she bobbed her nose up and down in what could have been encouragement.

"It's nothing to be ashamed of," Raoul said patronizingly, "there's no shame in only being able to ride one horse. You won everything on that grey when he was alive because he was talented, it takes a real rider to be able to duplicate that success on more difficult horses like that mare. Admit it, you just don't have what it takes."

"Her *name* is Allison," I said, pulling the mare's leather halter off her stall door, "not *that mare*. And she wouldn't let you ride her in a million years. Because you're an insensitive, rude, tactless lout who will never amount to anything if you don't learn to stop being a condescending ass."

There was silence as everyone stopped what they were doing to stare, and then Bethany suddenly burst into laughter.

"She's totally right, Raoul. You couldn't ride a horse like that, not properly."

"Well, she can't ride it, either," he snarled, but I'd already pulled Allison's blanket off and was running a soft brush over her silky bay coat. "I'd like to see her try."

"Fine," I said, brushing past him to get her gear out of the tack room. It was stupid to give in to a dare. I had a rule for myself never to allow angry emotions around when I was riding, but in this case, I just went with the momentum. I slid Allison's saddle and pad into place and lightly did up the girth.

She nickered in excitement when I put on her bridle and lipped at my jacket pocket for the peppermints she knew I kept there.

I took a deep breath and put on my helmet and gloves, then slid her stall open and walked her down the aisle past a sulking Raoul. Allison swished her tail hard as we went by, catching him on the cheek with the whip-like hairs.

"Stupid cow," I heard him hiss under his breath and I wasn't sure if he meant me or the horse. Probably both.

I didn't give myself time to second guess anything. From the corner of my eye, I saw Gil pull up Coconut and walk him on a loose rein to the far end of the ring. Coconut was a good, obedient stallion, but Allison didn't need any distractions tonight.

I was glad I'd let her play in the arena earlier today and hand-walked her, with any luck she would have worn some of that extra energy off.

I tightened the girth and slid into the saddle, but I didn't have much time to get used to the feeling before Allison was off, trotting like a rocket around the ring with her back tense and her nose in the air.

"Easy girl," I whispered, "just relax and breathe."

I let her stay in a trot but moved her in large circles, changing direction often, slowly asking her to bend and stretch. It took a while but gradually her tense muscles relaxed and she blew out a big breath of air. It wasn't long before I could ask her to move down to a walk and then back up to a trot again.

I was too focused on helping her to think about myself, and by the time we'd worked for forty-five minutes, we were both dripping with sweat but full of happiness.

"Good girl," I told her, sliding off her back and giving her another mint. The expression on her face was more relaxed than I'd seen in months. She'd truly missed having a job and working. I reached out and ran a hand down her neck, amazed at how good it had felt to be back in the saddle. I hadn't realized how badly I'd missed it.

Gil had disappeared at some point during my ride, but now he appeared again at my side and wrapped me in a hug, not saying a word. When he let me go, he patted Allison too, and we led her together to the wash stall for a well-deserved bath.

All the barn staff except Raoul were still there when I got back into the barn. I knew they'd all been watching my ride over the arena door but I didn't care.

"That was great, Jilly," Sonja said, "that's a nice mare and you can really ride. You didn't look afraid at all."

"I was never afraid," I said, "at least not of riding."

"Then why…?" Dora started but I cut in quickly, changing the subject before she could ask more questions.

"But what I *am* a little afraid of is sleeping in that big house alone tonight without even Betty being there. I do need to look into getting a dog."

"Well, you don't have to worry about that right now," Gil insisted, "you're not spending another night in that house alone. You're moving in with me until all this is over."

Sonja burst into laughter behind me. "Well, that's a nice way to ask a girl to live with you, studly, very smooth."

"Fine," he said gruffly. "It doesn't have to be with me as

long as she's somewhere safe. She can move in with the Hopps."

"Oh heck, no," Bethany said, "don't subject her to the Hopps and those giggling idiots. She'd probably do better taking her chances with the murderer."

"That's not funny," Sonja said quickly, "She can move into the staff house, then. We have a spare room."

"Yeah, if she doesn't mind freezing to death," Dora piped up from near the end of the aisle where she was brushing one of the brood mares." We're lucky to wake up alive every morning in that ice cube. Plus the stove still isn't fixed."

"Seriously?" I said in surprise. "Are you actually living without heat?"

"Well, Christoph said your mother promised to fix it," Sonja said, "but the repair man hasn't come yet and we can't use the woodstove because the top rusted out and it needs to be replaced. It's not so bad. We just sleep in our winter coats and pile on horse blankets. We assumed you knew."

"No, of course not, that's awful." *And if I'd been paying attention to what was going on in front of my face maybe I would have known it was happening*, I thought. *No wonder all our staff leaves after a season here. I'm pretty sure it's illegal to treat people like this.*

"Well, then it's solved," I announced, "I don't want to leave the house undefended anyway, the thieves could come back any time and I don't want them to have a second chance to steal something. And I don't want anyone freezing to death while I'm in charge. We have lots of rooms, and you're all welcome to stay in the manor until the heat is fixed."

There was a general cheer and the next hour was spent with everyone ferrying their meagre belongings into Greystone and getting settled in the spacious bedrooms. I didn't know if their heat situation had improved overly much since the unused rooms were damp and freezing, but I showed everyone how to light and take care of their fireplaces and where to find more wood in the storage room just outside of the back door. Mr. Hopps had been stocking my room with firewood all this time, but I couldn't expect him to cater to all these new people as well.

We filled the guest rooms on the bottom floor first and then Sonja and Nick took an upstairs one each, just down the hall from me. Despite my sudden loss of privacy, I was grateful to have the company. And Nick and Sonja and always been half-way decent to me.

Raoul hadn't exactly apologized for his behaviour earlier, but he had mumbled a gruff thank you for letting them move in there.

An hour later, he pulled up in front with one of the farm trucks and lugged out an old-fashioned television, not the flat-screened kind but the type that was about two feet thick and weighed sixty pounds.

"What?" he said looking at my doubtful expression. "There isn't even a radio in that place. Surely, you can't object to us watching T.V."

"It's not that," I said, heartily wishing that he hadn't moved over with all the others. It would have been nice to leave him behind to fend for himself. "I'm just not sure that it will work in here."

"Oh, stop fussing," he said ungratefully, "it'll be fine."

*Suit yourself*, I thought and was vindicated a while later when he tried to set it up in one of the sitting rooms and was rewarded with just bars of white static sliding across the screen.

"Stupid piece of junk," he grumbled, giving it a kick. "I'm so sick of having nothing to do in this town and on this stupid farm. It's just horses, horses, horses all day long."

"Well, you did move here to work as a rider on a *horse* farm," Sonja said, rolling her eyes, "so I'd say you knew what you were getting into."

I looked around the room, noticing their disappointed

faces. Everyone had gathered together expecting to watch a movie. Even though Raoul was being a big baby as per usual, there was no reason for the rest of them to suffer.

"We do have a few things for entertainment," I said slowly, clearing my throat a little nervously as they all swung their gazes toward me.

"Like what?" Bethany raised an eyebrow in my direction.

"Well, there's the pool, and the workout room and a hot tub and sauna, and the billiard room."

"Swimming," Dora said excitedly, "definitely a pool party."

I didn't have to say anything more, everyone leapt up and there was a mass exodus to find bathing suits and towels.

"You're the best, Jilly," Sonja said, hugging me as she passed. "Come on, aren't you getting your bathing suit?"

"No, you guys go on ahead, you don't need me there, I have some reading to catch up on anyway."

"No way, you can read any old time. You're coming with us, no excuses."

"I don't think Bethany and Dora would like it if—"

"Forget them, it's your house and you deserve to have fun, too. You were amazing to invite us over in the first place. Those girls are all right once you get to know them, they do like you, you know. Bethany was very impressed by the riding. Give it some time and you'll all be the best of friends."

Reluctantly, I let her drag me upstairs and push me toward my room.

"And text Gil to come over too while you're at it," she said, sending me a grin. "He'll be hurt if he misses a party."

"Oh, it's not a real party. I don't want to bother—"

"Honestly, Jilly, you're like the densest girl ever. If you don't start treating him better, you're going to lose him. Some other girl will swoop in and snap him up while you're still dithering. And I'm not ashamed to say that, if you don't get your act together, it might be me. He is a fine piece of real estate."

She sent me a saucy look over her shoulder and sauntered to her room.

*She's only joking*, I thought uneasily, but I pulled out my phone and sent him a text.

*Be right over*, he sent back and I hurried to change. I hadn't used my bathing suit in well over a year and I was out of shape after the accident, so it was a little tight to get into. It was a plain, navy one-piece but after it was on, I had to admit that it hugged my curves in all the right ways and brought out the blue in my eyes. I pulled my housecoat on overtop and padded down the stairs.

The hall was full of giggling and screeching girls and an embarrassed-looking Nick. Raoul strode around in his element wearing an alarmingly small yellow speedo and holding a bottle of whiskey in one hand.

"Um, you really shouldn't be drinking if you're going to swim," I said uncertainly, averting my eyes from the tiny scrap of fabric wrapped around his hips.

"Yeah, are you going to stop me?" he said in a teasing voice. He was smiling but the look in his eyes was downright vicious. "You think you're better than everyone just because you're rich. But I'm not going to be poor forever, Jillian, I have plans for my life. Big plans. Someday *I'm* the one who's going to look down on everyone. I'm going to be the powerful one."

"First of all, I'm not rich and I don't look down on anyone," I said, "and I can tell you now that you're not allowed to be drunk in this house or around the horses anymore."

"Yeah, and who's going to stop me?"

"You do realize that she can fire you," Gil said smoothly from behind me, "and so can I, or Christoph, or any one of us. You're not at all irreplaceable, you know."

"Whatever," Raoul said quickly, "we were just joking around. I'll put this away now, no harm done."

"Great," I smiled at him sweetly. "I'd hate for you to drown."

He shot me a look and went back to his room grumbling.

"I wish I could have left him behind," I said with a sigh, "he's going to be a lot to handle."

"Want me to stay over to keep an eye on him?" Gil asked. He said it like a joke, but there was a note of longing in his voice that made me take notice. I thought of him living all by himself in his loft and how he'd started hanging out in the staff house for company after I'd shut him out of my life.

"Would you?" I said gratefully, making a decision, "it would be nice to have some back-up here. I could use your help with this crew. I'm not used to dealing with people."

"Of course," he said in surprise. "All you had to do was ask."

"I know." I squeezed his arm. "Go on, get changed and I'll meet you at the pool."

The glassed-in room that held the pool was already echoing with squealing laughter by the time I got there. I'd turned the heat on earlier since the room only got used a few times a year when my family had guests and steam was rising upward, filling the air.

"It's so c-c-c-cold," Bethany said, her teeth chattering as she pulled herself out of the icy pool.

"Sorry, it will take a while to warm up. That's why there's a hot tub and a sauna," I laughed.

"G-g-g-g-g-good, idea." She ran past me and sank gratefully into the hot tub with a whimper of relief.

Suddenly, there was more squealing as a giant wave splashed over the far end of the pool, so high that it sloshed against the window and soaked everyone within a ten-foot radius.

"Raoul, you idiot, that's not funny," Sonja shrieked, grabbing for a towel.

"It wasn't me," he sputtered as he trod water in the middle of the pool, looking around nervously. "Someone jumped in beside me."

"Liar. You're the only one in there," she snapped.

He climbed out of the pool and looked around in bewilderment. "No, someone swam past me. I felt them touch my leg." He sounded almost frightened.

Everyone just ignored him, probably assuming he was either drunk or making up stories, but it was all I could do not to weep with laughter.

After all, I was the only one who could see Bally merrily paddling his way around the pool, snorting rhythmically with every stroke, water dripping off his ears.

*I didn't know you liked water*, I thought, *we'll have to make sure to take you swimming again when nobody else is around.*

I looked over and caught Gil watching me grin at an empty pool like an idiot and shrugged. It was no use; I didn't have the poker face necessary for leading a double life. I was just going to have to accept that sometimes people were going to think I was smiling and talking to myself like a crazy person. Even Gil.

Shaking off all my doubts, I leapt straight into the icy pool and swam laps beside the best ghost-horse a girl could have.

We all stayed playing in the pool and hot tub well into the night and I didn't think I'd ever been happier in my life. Part of my friend-starved soul just sort of lit up when I was surrounded by so many laughing people.

I didn't worry about not fitting in or belonging. I was just content to be myself, there with Gil and with people who'd accepted me for better or worse.

When I finally fell into bed that night, exhausted and happy, I thought that it had been the best time I'd ever had.

## Chapter 18

The next morning, Bally didn't wake me up for our pre-dawn walk as usual and it was my alarm that woke me up.

"Bally?" I asked, looking around the empty room but there was only Morris curled up in front of the dwindling fire. Even Nanny's chair was empty.

When I got to the barn ahead of everyone else, I was relieved to find him waiting not in his own empty stall but tucked in beside Damascus who looked exceedingly happy to have a friend.

"Are you two keeping each other company?" I asked, giving Damascus a scratch behind the ears.

They both tossed their noses up and down, making me burst into laughter. Saying "yes" was a trick I'd taught Bally when he was a youngster and it looked like Damascus had picked it up too somehow. They didn't know what I was asking them, they were just trained to answer anything that sounded like a question with a nose bob, but it looked cute.

Come to think of it though, maybe Bally *could* understand

me now. He seemed even smarter than he had been when he was living. And he'd always been a pretty brilliant horse.

"Morning, morning," the other grooms called out as they filed in one by one, yawning and rubbing their eyes.

"Jilly, there's no damn coffee," Sonja called out from the tack room, feigning outrage, "what's the number one rule of this barn?"

"First person out makes coffee," I said, laughing. "Look, don't drink that swill. There's better stuff at the house. I'll put some on as soon as I get back."

I whisked through my chores as fast as I could, eager to get back to the house and put on coffee so I could hide away in the library and look at Mr. Galinski's book again for a few minutes undisturbed. I was running out of time to find some answers.

But once I had the coffee freshly ground and bubbling in the stove-top percolator, it seemed a shame not to just whip up some scrambled eggs and bacon and maybe a little toast.

"What smells so good?" Bethany said, sailing in the kitchen door. "Wow, that looks amazing." She filled her plate and grabbed a coffee and began texting on her phone.

She must have sent out the word because in five minutes everyone had piled inside and was gathered around the stove, practically drooling in anticipation.

"We won't have enough for everyone unless we make pancakes, too," Raoul said, sending me an apologetic smile. He'd been on his most charming behaviour all morning. "My mother used to make the best, fluffiest pancakes in the world."

In no time the kitchen was full to capacity. As soon as the eggs were done, Raoul took over so I could eat and he could start on the pancakes. Morris made himself useful by jumping on the table whenever nobody was looking and sticking his face into everyone's plates.

"Your cat still doesn't have any manners, Jilly," Gil said as Morris was tossed to the floor for the third time.

"I know. I ruined a perfectly good barn cat," I said, scooping the big animal up and setting him firmly on my lap, out of trouble.

"Well, he's happy anyway. Do you want to help me when I ride Coconut? I could use some eyes on the ground while I work on his canter-pirouettes."

"Oh," I hesitated, thinking longingly of the document upstairs.

Just then there was a knock on the door and Katie poked her head inside. "Hey, is it okay if I ride today? There isn't any school and I don't have to work for once. I told my mom she could drop me off here. Wow, breakfast smells really good. Is there any left?"

I sighed heavily and put all thoughts of a peaceful morning of study aside. "Sure, Gil, I'll help you with Coconut. Katie, come on in and have some breakfast. If you help everyone clean stalls then you can spend the whole day riding."

"Oh my gosh, Jilly you're the best," she said, dropping her duffle bag by the door and heading to the stove, her eyes wide with anticipation.

"Hi," she said to Nick and Dora as she sat down beside them and began tucking into a plate of food. She did not seem the least intimidated by walking into a house full of strangers, although I noticed that she looked a little cautiously at Raoul.

After that, the day was full of horses. The usually quiet barn echoed with laughter and I found myself having more fun than I'd had in years.

Christoph looked at the cheerful grooms with astonishment and I felt a pang of guilt for not inviting him for breakfast that morning.

"Well, this is a nice change," he said, as everyone bustled to work.

"Yeah, well, we're not freezing for the first time in months," Bethany said, "and we actually had a decent night's sleep."

"Don't get too used to life at the big house," Christoph warned. "Mrs. Harrington will not be amused when she finds out about it. A repairman will be out to fix the heat this week."

Bethany made a face but said nothing.

"Oh, and Jilly," Christoph added, "I spoke to Betty and they want to keep her for the rest of the day but we can pick her up tonight."

"I hope she'll feel safe coming back to the house," I said, "it's horrible to be attacked in your own home."

"She's a strong woman. I'm sure she'll be fine. But you really should see about getting a better security system. At least until your mother gets back."

"I've always wanted a dog," I said thoughtfully, "I wonder if …"

"I don't think that's a good idea," Christoph interrupted quickly. "I believe that your mother had trouble adapting to the cat you brought home. Maybe a simple door alarm would be the best choice for now."

I smiled at him sweetly but secretly wondered how much longer Mother planned to be away. I was enjoying my freedom.

Katie brushed and tacked up Serena while I watched Gil warm up Coconut. The horse was a brilliant mover who performed at his best when Gil was on board, but today there was something a little off about him.

"His back looks a bit tight," I said thoughtfully, "how does he feel?"

"Almost perfect but it's as if he's holding back a bit. He doesn't feel quite sure of himself."

"I'd give him a couple of days off, Gil. And if he's still not doing well, we can get him seen by a chiropractor or massage therapist. What did Christoph say?"

"Same as you. He thinks Coconut is stiff from spending too much time in his stall. He's not used to it anymore after being at the trainers. They have covered paddocks there."

"I think they're all feeling it. I had an idea I meant to run past your dad." And I told him about my plan to get a load of sand brought in to make paths for walking and riding the horses carefully outside. "We could get enough to make some small paddocks for them to play in, too. Allison would really like getting outside, and I know Damascus and Bal... er, the rest of the horses are dying for a good play session."

"It's a good idea if your mother will agree to pay for it."

*Or, maybe I could use my own money once I come into my inheritance from Mr. Galinski. That way we wouldn't have to ask Mother at all.*

After that, I gave Katie her lessons on Serena and Lilo and then had her ride Lark for good measure.

"Whoa, she's different than the others," Katie said as Lark left the mounting block at a brisk walk, her pointy little ears swivelling in all directions.

"Yep, she's a sensitive, forward mare so you'll have to be prepared for quick, big movements. But, despite her energy, she's very sensible. I always liked riding her."

"Why don't you ride her anymore?" Katie asked, squeaking a little as Lark stepped up of her own accord into a brisk, ground-covering trot.

"You'd better just think about *her* while you're riding," I warned Katie. "You're going to need all your focus."

Katie nodded, already frowning in concentration. By the end of the lesson, she was smiling again though her cheeks were red with exertion.

"Oh my gosh, thank you so much for letting me ride her. For letting me ride them all. You have no idea how much this means to me."

"You're welcome. You can bath her and then put her away. There are still more stalls to do."

"And then you'll tell me what you found out about the book, right?" Katie whispered, looking over her shoulder to where Raoul was schooling one of the young horses.

"I can tell you what I know," I said slowly. "I have some questions for you too."

Katie cleaned stalls while I rode Allison and lunged Damascus, who were both on their best behaviour today. Allison was still a little tired from her ride the night before and I was already feeling muscles that I hadn't used in months. I would need a good soak in the hot tub again to ease my pain.

Katie and I went up to the house as soon as the stalls were all cleaned and our chores were done. We still had about an hour before the rest of the grooms would be looking hungrily for their lunch and I wanted to ask her some questions about Toby while nobody else was around.

Betty always kept the big freezer stocked with emergency rations and I pre-heated the oven before pulling out two big frozen lasagna's and setting them in to bake. I was probably supposed to thaw them first but I was pretty sure everyone would be too hungry to notice the difference.

I left Katie in the kitchen making herself a quick snack while I ran upstairs to get changed and find the book. I didn't need to change out of my barn clothes, but it was a good excuse to keep her from following me and seeing where I'd hidden the book.

I pushed aside the clothes in my closet to reveal the little half-hidden shelf behind. The concealed space was the next best thing to having a secret compartment. It was hard to see unless you were looking for it and the book stood up in there perfectly.

I pulled the book out, noticing what a calm and comforting presence it had. It didn't have that dark, oily feeling to it that Alocious's book had. This one felt like a good book.

*Which reminds me, I have to go and hunt for Alocious's missing book too at some point. I doubt it's really missing, but I should make sure.* Back at Dark Lady, the book had had the habit of turning up when it was least expected so I had a feeling I'd be seeing it again soon. Most likely the library ghost had taken it.

"Oh, there you are, finally," Katie said when I reached the library. "I've been waiting for ages."

"It's been like ten minutes," I told her.

"Well, it felt like forever. Do you know your Wi-Fi doesn't even work in this place?"

"Ah, yeah, I know." I set the book down and turned to the last page right away. We'd kept the two papers with the rubbings in them with the book and I arranged them carefully on the table so she could see.

"Katie. Do you recognize this?"

Her face went blotchy and instead of answering she covered her eyes and stifled a sob.

*I guess the answer is yes*, I thought, reaching out to put a comforting hand on her arm.

"Katie, it's okay, just tell me what you know."

"You weren't s-supposed … to see that. Nobody was. Toby thought … He tried …" She broke off in another fit of sobs.

"Katie, did Toby steal the page? Is that what he got fired for?"

"Yes." She hiccupped. "But he wasn't trying to do anything wrong. He was trying to protect everyone. He loved that book and he loved Mr. Galinski. He would have never … h-h-h-hurt him."

"Okay, but why rip out the page if he loved the book?"

"He said the page was bad. That it didn't belong with the book, and that someone was going to use it to do awful things. He said he had to get rid of it."

"Did he try and explain this to Mr. Galinski?"

"No, he was too embarrassed at getting caught with the book in the first place. Mr. Galinski had told him to leave it alone, but he said he couldn't help himself. Every time he saw it, he had to find a way to open it and read just a little bit. He showed it to me once when Mr. G had left us to mind the store."

"He could read it?" I asked skeptically, thinking of the strange symbols and pictures.

"That's what I wondered. It made no sense to me at all, either. But Toby said he could understand it perfectly. He loved that book; he was a bit obsessed with it."

"Hmm, so what did he do with the ripped-out page then?"

"I lost it." Her cheeks tinged pink and she looked away. "It was an accident."

"You lost it," I said blankly, "how?"

"Toby brought the page over to MapleBrew the day before Mr. Galinski was … was killed. We were discussing where to hide it. He wanted to destroy it, but he was worried that it was historically valuable or something. He's so crazy about books and history, that stuff is almost sacred to him."

Hmm, that fit in with what little I'd seen of Toby.

"We wanted to at least hide it somewhere safe until we figured out what to do, but then you came into the coffee shop and Toby got scared and ran. He's been so scared and jumpy for the last few weeks. It's like he became afraid of his own shadow. Anyway, the day got so busy after that. I slid it underneath the cash register until I could think of a good place to hide it. Then we got swamped with customers. By the time I looked again, it was gone."

Her shoulders sagged and she shook her head.

"I have no idea who could have taken it. Most of our customers are locals, and the grooms from your barn, I guess. I'm always so envious when they come in; they're so lucky to work here."

*Grooms from our barn*, I thought slowly. A few more pieces of the puzzle fell in place. *Raoul. That night I found him drunk in the barn he bragged about trading some old paper for money. I'll have to corner him and find out.*

Just then, the library door burst open and Sonja stuck her head in. "There you are, Jilly, lunch smells amazing. Did you already make garlic bread? We can't have lasagna without garlic bread."

Katie wiped her eyes quickly and stood up, clearly eager to end our conversation. "Is it okay if I stay for lunch? My mom can't pick me up until later in the day."

"Of course, there's enough for everyone. Do you happen to know how to make garlic bread by any chance?"

## Chapter 19

*L*unch was a huge success. Nick, amazingly enough, offered to make a Caesar salad and Katie did know how to make garlic bread so soon the kitchen was fragrant with delicious smells.

"This is so much better than instant noodles and sandwiches," Bethany said and there was a chorus of agreement.

Just then the kitchen door swung open and Christoph stood there with Betty on his arm.

"My word," she said, taking in the sea of people eating at her table. "What on earth is going on? Are you having a party?"

"Betty, they let you out early." I leapt up and came over to hug her. "I'm so glad you're okay."

"Well, they said I couldn't leave until I ate something," she said with a dark look, "but I couldn't touch their food. I'm only used to home-cooked. Finally, Christoph convinced me to eat some Jell-O just to appease them and that was good enough. They let me go."

"Oh, poor thing. You must be starving. Do you want me to bring a plate of something to your room for you?"

"No, I'm going to sit right down here at this table and have some of that nice lasagna and a piece of garlic bread. That smells heavenly right now. And then you're all going to tell me what's going on here."

Everyone shifted over so she and Christoph could have a spot, and I hurriedly made up plates for them.

"It isn't Jilly's fault we're here," Bethany said, "you can't get mad at her. Our heat went out and so did our oven. She brought us here so we wouldn't die. She's a hero."

"And honestly, I was too scared to stay here alone," I admitted. "It didn't feel safe."

"And she wouldn't move in with me when I asked," Gil added, appearing in the doorway. He winked at Betty and she smiled back at him. She'd always had a soft spot for Gil.

"Well, I don't mind myself. It's nice to have this house full of people again. I've been a little at loose ends without much of a job to do. But your mother is a different story. You know she wouldn't allow this if she were here."

"But she's *not* here," I said firmly, "and she doesn't have to find out about it." I sent a look at Christoph so he'd get my meaning. No tattling. "We just need to get the staff house renovated properly again and then everyone can move home. But until then, I say they stay."

That was the end of that argument, but as we were washing dishes, Betty pulled me aside. "You look so much happier dear," she said with a smile, patting my cheek. "You have a nice healthy glow for once. It's good to see you not looking so pale and sallow."

"Thank you," I said, hugging her. "I'm so glad you're home, and I'm sorry I haven't been much company for you lately. I've been selfish."

"You're not selfish dear, you've just had a lot to deal with. You know I've been with this family for a long time and I've seen a few things. You don't have to go through everything on your own. It's okay to ask for help and to reach out to people you trust."

I felt my eyes sting with tears. "I want to," I whispered, "but I'm scared to risk it."

"Oh, pshaw, you're not a coward, Jilly. You're strong and brave. And deep down you're a risk-taker. But you don't have to face the world all alone. Find a few people, a few *living* people, you can confide in. It's easier to bear a burden when you can share it."

*A few living people?* I stared at her in shock, then reached out and hugged her tightly. She'd known about the ghosts all along. Of course, she had. I'd been an idiot to think she wouldn't notice. I should have confided in her right from the beginning.

*I need to tell Gil everything soon*, I thought. *He's grown up here in this weird place and he's not afraid of it. He'll understand*

Everyone spent the next few hours lounging by the pool. And it was just like being on vacation. I couldn't remember any time in my life where I'd ever been this relaxed. All the tension I usually carried around just melted away.

The pool heat had finally kicked in and the water was perfect. Katie had dug out the blender and made us all custom fruit smoothies before she had to leave for work, and I thought I could get used to this new, luxurious lifestyle.

"My mom's here to pick me up," Katie announced. "But I'll be back tomorrow night after school to ride and help with chores."

"Thanks, Katie," I called from my lounge chair, "see you tomorrow."

## Chapter 20

*R*aoul did not show up to help Christoph with the young horses that afternoon and he didn't show up to do late-night chores, either.

"He's not in his room," Bethany called as she trotted back into the barn, "but all his stuff is still there."

"He's probably passed-out hungover somewhere," Sonja muttered, "he's been acting pretty strange lately."

*Oh great, we've lost another one,* I thought, although if we had to have anyone quit, I was glad it was Raoul. *I just hope he's not lying frozen in a snowbank somewhere. If he's not back soon, we'll have to have a search party.*

It wasn't until I got back to the house that something told me to go and check on Mr. Galinski's book.

*Oh, no, it can't be gone,* I thought, feeling around the hiding spot in my closet frantically. *Raoul couldn't have taken it. How did he have even known it was here?*

My phone chirped like a call was trying to get through and then the face went blank. The number that had flashed on the screen for a millisecond hadn't been familiar.

*I'd better go outside and see if someone is trying to reach me,* I thought when it chirped again. Greystone was having one of its limited cell reception days.

It rang properly the second I stepped back outside.

"Jillian?" a muffled voice said.

"Yes, that's me. Who is this?"

"It's Raoul. Um, I'm sorry. I sort of did something and … um, you're not going to like it."

"You took the book, didn't you?"

"Er, yes, that too—"

"Raoul, what's going on? Just bring the book home. Whatever you've done, we can sit down and talk it over with Christoph."

"No, no, I don't think I can do that. It's a little late." He made a choking, whimpering sound. "What I need you to do is meet me in town and bring that stupid knife with you. The real one."

"The knife? Raoul, I don't have any—"

"Oww." There was a scuffle in the background.

"Miss Harrington?" a cultured voice said. "There is no more time for games, I'm afraid. I have your, er … barn boy or whatever you call him … and I have Toby's little girlfriend here, too. If you don't bring me the knife by midnight, I'm afraid they'll both have to die."

"What? Who is this?"

"If you don't bring me the knife by then I will kill them both slowly. Piece by piece. And if you contact the police, I assure you I will know. I have eyes everywhere, Miss Harrington."

The line went dead and I froze, my thoughts whirling.

*Katie. He can't possibly have Katie.* I scrolled through my contacts and dialed her number but there was no answer. I hung up and called MapleBrew.

"Hello?" I recognized her cold voice right away.

"Kristal, it's Jilly. Did Katie make it to work this afternoon?"

"No, she didn't," Kristal's voice changed from frosty to worried. "Her mother swore she dropped her off outside and left her talking to some boy in front of the cafe. But she never showed up. She hasn't ever missed work before. I was just about to send out a search party. Do you know where she is?"

"No, but I'm working on it. I'll call you back." I hung up before she could ask anything else.

*Some boy outside the cafe? Would that have been Toby? Raoul? Think, Jilly, think.* A sensible person would call the police and let them deal with it, but what if I did that and then the murderer killed Katie and Raoul and it was all my fault? But I also couldn't bring him a knife I didn't have. Why did he think I had it anyway?

Suddenly there was a sort of popping sound, the air around me shimmered and Bally appeared. His eyes were wide and anxious and he whinnied at me with a piercing call. He pawed the ground hard and then trotted away a few feet. He turned to look at me and neighed again.

"Okay, Bally. It's okay, I'm coming."

I ran back inside and grabbed a coat and put on my boots before following him out into the snow. He trotted briskly across the snowy lawn in the direction of the barn and I followed him as best I could, my feet sinking into the half-melted drifts.

I flicked on the overhead lights and followed Bally down the aisle toward the hay room.

"What are we doing here, boy?" I asked, rolling back the door as quietly as I could. "It's not dinner time."

Bally didn't hesitate. He clambered up the rough staircase made by the bales of stacked hay and I followed more slowly, climbing the stack carefully. When I reached the top, I hesitated. At first, I didn't see anything but then there, in the far corner, I saw a quick flash of movement.

Was that … was that a person?

Bally snorted somewhere in the darkness and I followed the sound. He wanted me to see something and I had to trust that he wouldn't put me in danger.

As I drew closer there was a soft sniffling noise. I pulled out my phone and shone my flashlight into the dim reaches of the stack.

"Toby?" I said, recognizing him right away. He was huddled in the far corner under the eaves and despite the red blanket that he'd wrapped around his shoulders, he looked miserably freezing.

"Toby? What are you doing up here? You look half-frozen."

"K-K-K-K-Katie found this place for me to hide," he said, his teeth chattering. "I'm sorry."

"Come on, Toby, come to the house so you can get some food and warm up. We need to figure this all out and quickly."

"I c-c-c-can't," he said, "he'll kill me."

"Who will?"

"My dad. He's gone crazy."

"Your dad? What do you mean?"

"He killed Mr. Galinski. He stabbed him. I saw him do it. I saw you, too."

"How? Where were you?"

"Katie let me stay above the store after I ran away from my dad. He's … he's not right in the head. He got sick last year and ever since then he's been obsessed with finding a way to live forever. He made me steal things from school.

He pretended to be friends with Mr. Galinski, and he tried to get me to spy for him and to steal the book. But he wanted it for all the wrong reasons. The book said that I needed to tear the last page out, the page that talked about the knife, because without it my dad wouldn't know what to do. He couldn't read the book like I could. The book let me understand."

"What do you mean the book let you?"

Toby shrugged. "I don't know. At first, it just all looked like nonsense, but when I touched it, I could understand."

I stared at him wondering how much of his rambling speech was just due to hypothermia.

"Come on, let's get to the house. You can tell me the rest there. I have to find Katie and Raoul."

"He's got her, doesn't he?" Toby said brokenly as he crawled across the top of the hay after me. "He said he'd kill her if I didn't listen to him. He wants the knife."

*He wants the knife.* I waited until Toby had climbed unsteadily down to the ground. He looked sick and cold, and I wondered how long he'd been up there.

"Katie brought me up here after the … after I saw Mr. Galinski get killed. We didn't know where else to go. If my dad found me, he was going to kill me, too."

"Katie? How on earth did she smuggle you into Greystone?"

"She used her mother's car. Her mother takes a lot of pills to sleep and she doesn't notice what Katie does anyway a lot of the time."

We made it to the house and I ushered him inside, hurrying him toward the fire.

"That was days ago, Toby. How did you survive up there in the cold? How did you eat?"

He shrugged and sank gratefully to the floor in front of the fireplace. I was worried for a moment that he'd try to crawl inside. He closed his eyes and sighed, and I could practically see him thawing before my eyes.

"I was pretty out of it the first day. I guess I was in shock. Katie left me with some granola bars and stuff, but she couldn't get up here for a while because of the police and everyone crawling around. It was really cold and I buried myself in the hay but I still pretty much thought I'd die."

He looked down at the red blanket still wrapped around him and frowned. "Then this old lady showed up. She gave me this blanket thing and said she wouldn't tell anyone I was here. I never saw her again but after that, bits of food would just show up beside me. I found a lot of apples and one day there were some eggs. No plate or anything, just the food."

*Nanny and Bally*, I thought in astonishment. So that's what they'd been up to. They'd been taking care of Toby all this time. But why couldn't they have just told me he was here?

"I'm sorry I stole the knife from you," he said suddenly. "It's all my fault Mr. Galinski died. He was so nice to me too."

"You took it? And you replaced it with the fake?"

"Yeah. Dad has been obsessed with the Serpent's Blade for a long time. He studies history and he has a special interest in Alchemy and he'd found this stuff about a knife that could be used to hurry up the process to make the Elixir of Life. It didn't take him long to discover that your family had one of the blades. There are only a few left in the world, you know. And only two in North America. He'd planned on taking yours ever since he realized that the knife he'd made me steal from school was a fake. It was just luck that your family happened to live in the same town as his old friend Mr. Galinski."

*Not exactly luck*, I thought grimly.

"I didn't think you'd even notice it was gone. My dad said I had to get it for him or he'd kill me. I snuck in and took it while you were riding horses with Katie."

*Wow. Really?* "Did Katie know you'd stolen it?"

"Um," he shifted around uncomfortably. "She knew that I was in trouble and she was trying to protect me. We thought that if we just got the knife for my dad that he'd go away. I had no idea he'd use it on Mr. G. or I would have never stolen it in the first place."

"But Toby, you knew he had to kill *someone* with the blade for the Elixir thing to work. You knew that if he had the knife he'd use it for murder. Yet you gave it to him anyway."

"Yeah, I know. I'm not proud of that. I guess I hoped he'd never go through with it. It isn't like he's killed anyone before. I tried to steal the page from the book so at least he couldn't figure out how to use the knife properly but that backfired too.

Honestly, I was scared and wanted him out of my life so I could start over. I figured he wouldn't bother me anymore once he got what he wanted. I left the knife for him in our hotel room and then grabbed my stuff and ran. Katie hid me above the coffee shop and we thought I could just stay there until my dad left town. Only, it didn't turn out that way."

"You saw the murder from the coffee shop window, didn't you?"

He nodded. "From upstairs, you can see right into the bookstore. I saw my dad fight with Mr. Galinski and then stab him. I ran downstairs to try and help him but just then, you sort of … appeared out of nowhere so I hid until you were both in the back of the store.

I snuck in and tried to get Mr. G to wake up but it was already too late. He was gone. But I knew there was one thing I could do. I knew why my dad had left the knife in poor Mr. G and I just couldn't let that happen. It was awful but … I pulled the knife out and ran. When I was back upstairs, I called the police and then called Katie. She smuggled me out and brought me to Greystone. The whole thing was awful."

"Here," I said, handing him a plate of leftovers that I'd warmed in the microwave.

He took it gratefully, the fork trembling between his fingers as he shovelled food into his mouth as fast as he could.

"So, since you've had the real knife all along then why did you break in here and steal the fake one back again?"

"Huh?" he said. "I don't know anything about that. I

haven't moved from that corner of the hayloft since I got there. I was too afraid to do anything."

"Toby," I said, "you need to give me the knife now."

"Oh, sure," he fumbled under his blanket and then tossed a solid object wrapped in layers of paper towel onto the floor. It hit the tile with a dull thud. "Don't worry, I washed it in the sink. It's clean. You can have it. I don't ever want to see it again. Once you have Katie back, we should destroy it. That's what the book said to do."

"The book said that, huh?" I said, picking up the wrapped knife and shoving it into my coat pocket before he could change his mind. I looked at him, concerned, not liking the sheen of sweat that now glistened across his forehead. He did not look well at all.

"Yep, and it said that I could trust you, too. Can you let Katie know that I'm okay when you find her? She's been so worried about all this."

*If I find her in time*, I thought grimly.

I led Toby to Raoul's old room since I wasn't sure if he would make it up the stairs, and then I ran to get Betty. I didn't have to tell her everything, she took one look at him and ordered him to get tucked into bed and she found an old pair of my father's warm flannel pajamas to put on.

I left her fussing over him and hurried to my room to look at the knife.

*Yes, it's the right one,* I thought, staring down at the hated blade. *I can't wait to destroy this thing.*

So, what was I to do next? My first instinct was to call Gil, but if he thought I was walking into danger then he'd never let me go. He'd call the police first thing and then Katie might be killed.

But I didn't want to be walk in and blindly face a murderer, either.

"You're running out of time, Jillian," Nanny said suddenly, appearing in her rocking chair.

"Jeesh," I said, "nice of you to show up. When were you planning to tell me you were harbouring a fugitive in the barn?"

"Oh, right. Well, Jillian, that boy needed our assistance and telling you where he was at the time wouldn't have helped anyone."

"Um, actually it would have helped quite a—"

"Ah, ah"—she held up a hand— "do not argue with me when you know I'm right, Jillian. Bally and I knew how to keep him safe. Now it's time for you to do your part. Get Katie back and destroy that blade once and for all."

I gulped, suddenly overwhelmed with fear. Why was this all on *me* to take care of? I couldn't go up against a murderer.

My phone chirped in my pocket and I picked it up only to have it die again.

Damn this house.

I ran down the stairs and out the front door as fast as I could. It rang again almost instantly.

"Do you have what I need, Jillian?"

It was Professor Mason, his voice sounding strained beyond belief.

"It is nowhere near midnight yet," I said, stalling for time.

"Plans have changed. Meet me at the bookstore in twenty minutes. If you're late, this kid dies. Bring the knife."

The line clicked dead and tears sprang to my eyes. What was I going to do?

I ran upstairs to my room again.

"Nanny, if I do this … if I go, will you please find a way to tell Gil where I am? Will you get him to call the police once I'm already there and I've made sure that Katie and Raoul are safe?"

"Oh well, I can do my best." She didn't sound too

convinced. She looked down at the knitting in her lap, now a new blue blanket rather than the red one she'd been working on for the last few months.

"Nanny, you can do this," I said firmly. "Come on, I need you to help me. I know you and Bally took care of Toby and I know you've helped me before. Just promise me you'll try."

"Of course, dear," she said, looking vaguely off in the distance, "we'll be there when you need us."

And with that, she disappeared.

I was out of time.

## Chapter 21

*M*yrtle started up after a token protest, and I shoved her into drive without even letting her warm up.

The garage doors shut behind me with a bang as soon as I'd backed out into the snow, my shed-ghost seeming more agitated than usual.

My hands shook the whole way into town. I didn't have a plan, I didn't have any backup, and I wasn't sure if the ghosts would help me in time.

The bookstore was shrouded in darkness when I got there, there was no moon to light my way tonight, and the streetlight out front had burnt out, leaving that whole section of the street in shadow. *How convenient.*

The front of Curiosity was unguarded. There was no sign of Billy and I wondered worriedly if something had happened to him. Had Toby's dad gotten to him, too?

I had to force myself toward the front door, every inch of my body urging me to run in the opposite direction.

*Think of Katie and Raoul, they're depending on you.*

Glass crunched under my boots as I slowly opened the front door to the book shop.

*Not just any book shop*, I reminded myself, *Curiosity is my place now, it belongs to me and it's up to me to defend and protect it.*

I gritted my teeth and pushed my way forward, letting the door close softly after me. I pulled the flashlight out of my pocket and flicked it on, the beam cutting through the inky blackness.

*Oh, no, Katie.*

She was curled up on the floor, her long hair covering her face. I couldn't tell if she was living or dead. Billy lay stretched out on the floor beside her, his head tilted awkwardly to one side. And beside him, Raoul sat tied to a wooden chair. He had a livid bruise on his face and one eye was swollen shut. He was awake, though. He followed my progress with his one good eye.

"Jilly," he said in a croaking voice, "I'm so sorry, I never meant for any of this to happen. I just needed the money. I had no idea he'd hurt anyone. He just said he needed the knife and the book."

"You broke in and stole the knife the other night, didn't you?" I asked as realization dawned. "You hit Betty over the head."

"It was an accident. I didn't expect her to walk in."

"And Katie? Did you lure her in here, too?"

"He promised he wouldn't hurt her. She's just sleeping like that cop over there. He needs the knife, Jilly. I brought him the wrong one I guess, and he had to hurt me. Just give him what he wants and we can all go home."

"Hello, Jillian," a cold voice said out of the darkness.

I pulled my gaze away from Raoul and looked toward where Toby's dad was standing.

"Professor Mason," I said as my light flashed across him. He looked awful. Gone was the suave, confident persona of before. He looked like he hadn't bathed in weeks and his hair stood up in all directions. A smear of what was probably blood covered one cheek. He looked like a dying, desperate man.

"Yes, that's me. Did you bring the knife?"

"I did. I said I would. Now let them go."

"Not until I see it," he said, rubbing his filthy hands together as he took a few stumbling steps toward me, "let me see it."

I moved back toward the door and pulled the knife slowly out of my pocket. Maybe I could lure him outside …

But as soon as he saw the knife, something snapped inside of him, and he leapt toward me so fast I barely had time to throw myself out of the way. Grasping fingers tore at my arm, wrenching the knife out of my hand and pushing me hard to the floor.

My flashlight clattered onto the hardwood and lodged itself beside a fallen bookshelf, lighting up the spot where Raoul, Katie and Billy were.

Mason was on me in an instant. I saw the blade come at me, but I managed to kick him hard and roll out of the way. There was a scraping, thumping sound and I saw Raoul bouncing up and down in his chair, trying his best to move it toward me.

I scrambled in that direction, but Mason was too fast. He cut in front of me, his eyes glinting in the low light. He stood facing me, his back to Raoul, a murderous smile lit up his face.

With a muffled cry Raoul threw his chair over, hitting the man in the back of the knees as he fell. Mason stumbled off-balance, and I leapt toward him, pushing him hard so he fell backward over Raoul's toppled body.

He half-turned toward me as he fell, swiping out with the knife so I just felt the razor-sharp tip of it graze my throat. I clapped my hand against my skin and ran toward the front of the shop just as the door burst open and the police poured inside.

I stood with my back against the wall and watched with disbelief as they swarmed toward the man. It had worked, it had actually worked, I'd stopped Mason and now everything was going to be okay. He would go to jail and....

"Noooo," Mason let out a defeated groan and I could hear him gasping for air.

"Ambulance," one of the officers barked, "we need medics in here now. Multiple victims here and we have an officer down."

"It's not my time," Mason wheezed from behind the wall of officers, "I'm not ready. There's still so much to do."

I craned my head, trying to see what was happening with Mason. Why weren't they hauling him outside into a police car?

I could see other officers untying Raoul and hovering over Katie and Billy but I felt strangely removed from the scene. As if it were happening in a dream and not in real life. The adrenaline from my adventure was fading and I was left only with exhaustion.

I sank to the ground, leaning heavily up against the wall, my hands still clamped over the wound on my neck. It hurt now, and I wondered dimly if I would need sutures or if it would leave a scar.

"I don't want to go. I want to live... forever." Mason's voice broke off with a gurgle and there was a dull thump as his head hit the floor. From my new position, I could see directly into his now-vacant eyes. And I could see further down, the glint of the blade buried in his chest from where he'd fallen on it.

*Oh,* I thought dimly, *that's not how it was supposed to end. And why am I so cold?*

I glanced down and saw that my arm was slick with blood to the elbow and that my shirt was soaked.

*That's funny*, I thought, blinking slowly, *it seems like a lot of blood for just a little scratch. I think I'm just going to lie down and have a nap. I'll wake up again when it's all over.*

"Jilly!" Gil's voice came from so far away that I barely heard him. "We need an ambulance here, someone. You're fine, Jilly. I'm right here. Stay with me. Don't go."

The cold faded and was replaced with a delicious warmth that surrounded me. The darkness brightened and all around me was a soft, glowing light. Like being inside a warm, dry cloud. I heard a soft snort and felt Bally's whiskers tickling my cheek.

Beyond him, I could sense other ghosts. Some nearby and others further away. Hundreds of them turning their focus on me all at once, moving toward me in an unending wave.

*There are too many*, I thought, feeling a stab of anxiety, *I can't help them all by myself.*

Bally touched my face reassuringly and that feeling of peace flooded over me once again. I was drifting away slowly, moving steadily toward the light.

"Jilly, don't leave me." Gil's voice came again, more desperate this time.

*I can't leave Gil*, I thought dimly. *Not yet.* And with a rush the cold and pain came rolling back.

## Chapter 22

"You're such a cheater," I said, throwing down my cards in a huff. "That's the fifth time in a row you've won."

"That's not cheating, that's just called being good at cards." Gil plucked the deck from off the table and began shuffling again. "One more time?"

"Sure." I sighed. "Why not. It's not like I'm allowed to do anything else right now."

Because of the blood loss and my near-death experience, I had been on strict bed rest for a week after being released from the hospital. Which seemed ridiculous since I felt perfectly fine. I was anxious to get back to doing my own barn work and riding my horses. At least it felt good to *want* to ride again.

"Katie's going to hate it when you're back. She's loving all the extra riding. Christoph thinks we should keep her on permanently."

"I agree. She's welcome to stay as long as she wants. I'll just keep riding Allison and help Christoph with starting the babies. It's the least I can do since it's partly my fault Raoul got himself arrested and fired. At least they're sending him back home to his family."

Even though he'd often been a vile person I still felt bad for Raoul. He'd been the one to stop Professor Mason in the end and I hoped he'd find a way to turn his life around once he'd returned home. He'd also confessed to stealing several trinkets from the house, including my ancestor Alocious's book from the library. He'd had it stashed away in his room although he'd sworn he hadn't had time to read it.

It was safely locked up in the archives room now and that's where it would stay for a good long while.

"How is any of that your fault?" Gil said, startling me out of my thoughts.

"Well, if I'd stepped in earlier to make their living and working conditions better, maybe he wouldn't have been so angry and desperate. I shouldn't have been so caught up in my own world that I wasn't paying attention to what was happening around me."

I reached up to scratch the bandage on my neck and then stopped when Gil gave me a look.

"No scratching," he said, "doctor's orders."

"Yeah, yeah, I know." It was a good sign that it was itching because that meant that the gaping neck wound they'd repaired was healing properly, but at the same time, the stitches drove me crazy.

A scent of lavender filled the room and I looked up, blinking as a faint apparition partially materialized.

*Wow, I can see Library Ghost,* I thought in astonishment, *kind of.*

I couldn't make out her features but I could see that she was there hovering in the corner about six feet off the ground.

Gil looked up and then glanced over his shoulder to see what I was staring at.

"Mila the library ghost?" He asked casually.

I froze and stared at him.

"How... how do you know that?" I asked in astonishment. "And how do you know her name?"

"I grew up with you, Jilly," he said patiently. "I know you lost a bunch of your memories. But I didn't lose mine. You didn't keep secrets from me when you were a kid. You told me everything. Of course, I know about the damn ghosts."

He tossed the cards down and stared at me, arms crossed over his chest.

"You're the one who refused to talk about them after we nearly drowned, Jilly, not me."

My breath came out in a gasp as I released the air from my lungs. I couldn't believe I'd been so stupid as to forget all this.

"No way. I told you about them? Did you believe me at the time? Did you think they were real?"

"They were real to *you* and that's what mattered the most," he said slowly. "But also, I'm not blind. Greystone has always been a weird place. Things falling over randomly, strange smells and sounds. The feeling that something was watching me. Something other than your creepy mother, I mean. The ghost thing just made sense when you explained it."

"So, wait, I told you who some of these ghosts were then? Like I gave you names and descriptions?"

"Yeah, I mean I can't remember them all; we'll need to find your notebooks if you want all the details. You wrote everything down. But I know the library ghost is Mila who was a paid companion for one of your ancestors. And the guy in the shed was a gardener. I think his name was Nate or something."

"Wow, this is amazing, Gil. I can't believe that you knew this all along. I've been such an idiot not to tell you in the first place."

Gil raised his eyebrows and did not disagree with me.

"Did I ever tell you about the weird dreams I've been having?" He said finally.

"Dreams? No, I don't think so."

"On the morning you found Mr. Galinski, I had this strange nightmare, right before your mother called from halfway across the world to let us know you were in trouble."

"Did you?" I asked slowly, wondering where this was going.

"Yes, it was about Bally actually, and it seemed very real. He came to tell me that you were in trouble. It woke me up out of a sound sleep. I was convinced that you were involved in some sort of emergency in town. I was already dressed and ready to drive to the bookstore to rescue you when your mother called."

"Oh," I said, an intense feeling of relief washing over me.

"And then your mother rang and started barking orders at Christoph, and when my dad asked how she knew that you were in trouble, she just said that she'd had a dream about a horse."

"Yeah ... about that," I said, but he held up a hand to cut me off.

"And I had another dream about Bally right when you headed back to the bookstore to confront Professor Mason. I hadn't even realized I'd dozed off, but I woke up so convinced that you were in danger that I called the police without even hesitating."

"Gil," I choked on a sob. "Bally is…"

"I know," he said quietly. "I've guessed for a while now."

"You never said anything." I sniffled, wiping my tears away.

"No, because you seemed determined to do everything on your own. To shut me, and everyone else who could help you, out. You never asked for help."

I hadn't. Not once. I'd dealt with my churning emotions and my fear all by myself. Just like I'd done since I was a teenager.

"I… I'm sorry, Gil," I said. "I thought I was protecting you."

"Well don't. That's over now. We're a team, Jilly. Where you go, I go. No more secrets."

"No more secrets," I agreed, reaching out to take the hand he offered me.

He smiled and shifted his fingers so they were linked with mine, threaded together firmly. Just like they belonged that way.

## Chapter 23

*W*e all came out to send Toby off on the day he left for school. His mother had come to get him; she'd been kept away for years by his domineering father and had been delighted to see her son again. Even if it was only to spend a few hours with him before dropping him off at a fancy boarding school.

He walked slowly to the car, holding Katie's hand tightly in his. He'd spent three weeks recovering at Greystone from the shock of his father's death and from battling a case of pneumonia. But in that time he'd blossomed into a happy, confident teenager. He looked like a different person from the scrawny, nervous boy I'd first met.

"Thank you for everything," he said to me, reaching out to shake my hand, "you saved my life."

"Of course," I said, pulling him into a quick hug. "And I'll keep the book safe for you until you get back. It will be waiting here for you. I know that's what Mr. Galinski would have wanted."

"Thanks," he said again and looked away. "And the blade is gone for sure? And the page?"

"I burned the page myself," I promised. "And we watched the Serpent's Blade get melted down right in front of us and we threw what was left away."

Gil was good friends with the farrier who shod our horses and he'd used his forge to melt down the blade and the hilt. And we destroyed the fake Serpent's Blade at the same time. No point in having it around for anyone else to try and steal. I wasn't looking forward to explaining the whole thing to Mother, though.

We'd taken the disjointed metal blobs that were left and had thrown them in different garbage cans at various nearby towns. Nobody would ever be able to use the Serpent's Blade for evil again. Without the page to guide them, I hoped that nobody would associate whatever remaining knives still existed in the world with Alchemy at all.

"Bye, Katie," he said, hugging her close and then kissing her gently on the lips. "I'll be back for the holidays, I promise."

"I know you will," she said, but she had to turn away as he got into the car so he wouldn't see her crying.

She waved at the departing car and then sighed heavily as it turned the corner and disappeared.

"Come on," I said, "time to get to the store. We promised to meet everyone there."

We'd all decided together that the best way to get over the awful things that had happened at Curiosity was to clean it up and get it looking like Mr. Galinski would have wanted again. That store had been his life and I didn't want it to be tarnished by the legacy of that madman Mason.

I wasn't sure what I was going to do with the store yet, but I'd decided to take it one day at a time and just see what happened next.

By the time we got there, the official clean-up crew had already been in to take care of all the blood and to make sure it was safe to return to. But there was still plenty to do. All the bookshelves had to be put back up and the broken doors replaced and the glass swept up and repaired.

"I thought you might be able to use some coffee and treats," a hesitant voice said from behind me.

"Aunt Kristal," Katie said in delight and gave my arm a little shove. "Look, Jilly, she brought your favourite cinnamon buns. Wasn't that nice of her?"

"Er, yes, thank you," I said, "you didn't have to do that."

Kristal wasn't dressed to the nines for once. She had on jeans and a plaid jacket and had her hair pulled back in a messy ponytail. I hardly recognized her.

"Yes, yes I did. You saved Katie and you saved Billy and Toby. You're a hero, Jilly, and I want to apologize for the way I've treated you in the past. I was just ... when you talked about ghosts—"

A deep blush stained her cheeks.

"It was kid stuff," I said hastily, laying a hand on her arm. "It was in the past. Let's just forgive and forget, okay? We can start over."

Kristal opened her mouth as if to say something and then shut it again abruptly. "Sure," she said finally. "Now show me how I can help clean up this place. Since we're going to be neighbours and all, I can't have you bringing the tone of the neighbourhood down."

*Same old Kristal*, I thought, as I handed her a broom. *Still, I wonder why my ghost stuff bothered her so much when we were kids?*

It was something to think about later when there wasn't so much work to do.

Everyone from Greystone had come to help, and with all of us crammed into the little shop, it didn't take long for things to take on a semblance of order again.

"I'm not sure how this part got destroyed, though," I said as Katie and I worked on carefully cleaning up all the smashed glass in the old laboratory. "The door was shut when

I was hiding in the office and I had the key. Nobody came in."

"I think Mr. Galinski must have done it himself," Katie said thoughtfully. "That's what Toby thought anyway when I told him the story. He said that Mr. G would have done anything to protect his secrets from Mason once he knew what he was up to. He destroyed his experiments so the Professor couldn't have them."

"Yeah, that makes sense, you're probably right."

"Miss Harrington," a jovial voice said behind me, "it's good to see you looking well and up and about. Putting the old place in order, are you?"

"Detective Anderson," I said, turning to greet him. But my greeting turned into a delighted squeal when I saw the fluffy bundle in his arms.

"Ooh, did you adopt one? Is this from the shelter your sister works at? She's adorable."

"It's a he, actually. His name is Rufus right now, but he's so young that he'll come to anything you decide on."

"Wait, what?" I said as he shoved the squirming black puppy into my arms. I couldn't say anything else because I was busy protecting my face from some enthusiastic washing.

"He's a Labrador mixed with a little Husky mixed with maybe some Newfoundland, so he should end up big and friendly. A perfect mix of guard dog and pet."

"Oh, no," I said quickly. "I can't keep him. Mother would—"

"She'll get used to the idea eventually," Gil interrupted, giving the puppy a scratch behind the ears. "I think he's perfect. Greystone's needed a dog for a long time."

"Are you perfect?" I asked the puppy and was rewarded when he nipped me gently on the nose. "We'll have to think of a good name for you then I guess."

The pup squirmed in my arms and I walked over to the

little alcove and set him down on the ground so he could explore.

He dropped his nose to the floor, making a little snuffling noise as he followed a scent toward one of the bookcases.

"What are you looking for buddy?" I asked, laughing as he ran his nose up the shelf. "Are you hunting something?"

*Hunter? Would that be a good name for him?*

He sat down abruptly, his little tail wagging back and forth as he looked at something over his head.

A light breeze ruffled his fur and then ran across my arms.

*A ghost? Could it even be Mr. Galinski?*

The dog whined a little and then dropped his nose again, sniffing his way happily over to the next shelf.

No, not Hunter. *Seeker.* A seeker of truth, a solver of mysteries. The perfect sidekick for my far-from-normal life.

"How does Seeker sound, buddy?" I asked softly, looking up as Gil came in and laid a hand on my shoulder.

A gentle thud sounded beside me and Bally appeared next to the couch, staring down at the new puppy eagerly with his ears pricked.

*My family,* I thought, suddenly filled right to the brim with happiness. For the first time in my entire life, I had exactly everything I needed. And, despite all the heartbreak and chaos I'd endured, I wouldn't change a single thing.

I couldn't wait to see what happened next.

The End (For Now)

## Acknowledgments

Thanks to my mother for sparking my love of mysteries, puzzles and enigmas. Every birthday and Easter morning I'd wake up with a clue taped to my pillow (or sometimes my forehead) leading me on a hunt to find my presents. The adventure was always half the fun.

## About the Author

Genevieve McKay is the author of over a dozen books, and most of them are about horses. She is an avid rider, reader, tea-drinker, and solver of mysteries. She lives on the west coast of Canada with her family, her horses, and an assortment of barnyard animals such as dogs, cats, sheep, chickens and two half-tame ravens.

# Also by Genevieve Mckay

If you are enjoying the Greystone Manor series, Defining Gravity series or any of my other books, I'd love if you'd take a moment to write a review on Amazon, Goodreads or any of the platforms where they are sold.

You can keep in touch by;

Visiting my website at www.genevievemckay.com

Follow my pics on Instagram: @mckaygenevieve

Or join my Facebook author page: www.facebook.com/authorgenevievemckay

I also have a mailing list where you can stay up to date on new releases, promotions and giveaways.

https://landing.mailerlite.com/webforms/landing/d2s9l0

## Greystone Manor Mysteries

The Curse of the Golden Touch

The Sting of the Serpent's Blade

The Skull on the Crooked Road (Coming Soon)

## The October Horses series

The October Horses

Facing the Fire

Keeping Chilly (Coming soon)

## Defining Gravity series

Defining Gravity

Flight

Freefall

Riding Above Air

Touching Ground

Three Sisters Farm Series

Everyday Horses

Odd One Out (Coming Soon)

Short Stories and Collections

The Horses of Winter